I0796800

CROCHET HOW

simple stitches, patterns, and tips

Meghan Fernandes & Lydia Gluck
creators of Pom Pom

abrams, new york

CONTENTS

Find *Crochet How* tutorials on our YouTube channel: www.youtube.com/@PomPomPublishing and crochet along with us!

INTRODUCTION

You probably have an inkling of this, since you're reading this book, but crochet is mind-blowingly amazing. First fun fact: Crochet can't be replicated by a machine. Knitted stitches can, and there are ways to create fabric that looks a bit like crochet on a machine, but true, actual crochet cannot. In this day and age, that's pretty special. By learning to crochet, you're joining a group of people who have the unique power to do something that a machine can't. See? Mind-blowing, right?

Fun fact #2: Being a crocheter is kind of like being a human 3-D printer, except you, the human, get to have fun while "printing." Crochet is wonderful because, of all the types of fabric making, it's the easiest to make three-dimensional. Crochet stitches don't have to be made going all in one direction, like weaving and most knitting does. Even in its simplest form, you can go forward, backward, sideways, up, and down with relative ease. Magic.

So, welcome! We are so happy you're here, joining this legion of makers who get to make whatever we want, with our own hands . . . and yarn and a hook, of course. In this book, we'll be with you every step of the way, as you start your very first stitches, through to simple accessories, and all the way up to garments and amigurumi. You don't need to have any knowledge about crochet right now. We're going to start from absolute scratch. But if you do, or if you're even already a knitter, for example, this book will still help you understand lots of concepts and is a treasure trove of tips and inspiration that will be a lovely companion throughout your crafting life.

Let's jump in. Hooks at the ready!

xo
Lydia + Meghan

PART 1

USEFUL THINGS TO KNOW

BEFORE WE GET STARTED

OK, deep breath—we're jumping in. A few things to remember before we get started.

practice
You're going to want to do some practice crochet before you start an actual project. This means taking some yarn and a hook and fiddling around until said yarn looks like crochet fabric. This might take a little while. Throw your perfectionist tendencies out the window for now; your crochet is probably not going to look very pretty to start with. It might be an odd shape. There might be holes. It might be loosey-goosey or it might be tight as armor, but it'll get better, we promise. This is all about practice. And as we always say, being bad at something is the first step to being really good at something.

how stitches are made
Traditional crochet (the kind in this book) only ever has one live stitch, regardless of the size of the fabric you are making, which gives you a lot of freedom. One of the amazing things about crochet (and there are many) is how sculptural it can be, and how many different stitch patterns can be created with it. It lends itself to lace and 3-D shapes like nobody's business. For now, we'll concentrate on a few basic stitches. Most of the other ones are very similar to these.

All basic crochet stitches are made up of a set number of loops pulled through other loops. They vary in how many loops you pull through to create a little stack (which is akin to a knot of sorts) before you move on to your next stitch. One of the other interesting things to know about crochet is that it uses a lot of chain stitches, single loops of yarn pulled through one another, which often form the beginning of a piece of fabric, help us start a new row or round of stitches, or create decorative or functional eyelets in our fabric.

how to get your supplies
You can find a crocheter friend to borrow a hook and yarn from (crocheters are nice like that), or if you're ready to invest, we suggest heading to your local yarn shop (aka LYS in crochet-speak).

international terminology
If you're in the UK, Europe, or Australia, you'll be looking for a 5- to 6-mm hook and some Aran or chunky weight yarn. They'll know what you're talking about at the yarn shop. In the US, you'll ask for size H, I, or J hooks and worsted to bulky weight yarn. (Like imperial and metric measurement systems, there are still different conventions for sizing hooks and yarn in different countries. See cover flaps for handy conversion tables!) If you want to order supplies online, the same terms apply. And if you want our personal recommendation for great starter supplies, we love Kremke Soul Wool's The Merry Merino 70 yarn and an ergonomic hook (with a comfy handle) in size 6 mm/US J, such as Clover, Tulip, or Prym brand. Once you've got some yarn and a hook, you can get going.

you will need:

(UK, EUROPE, AUSTRALIA)
5–6 mm crochet hook
Aran or chunky weight yarn

(US)
Size H, I, or J crochet hook
Worsted or bulky weight yarn

GETTING STARTED: KNOTS, CHAINS, AND STITCHES!

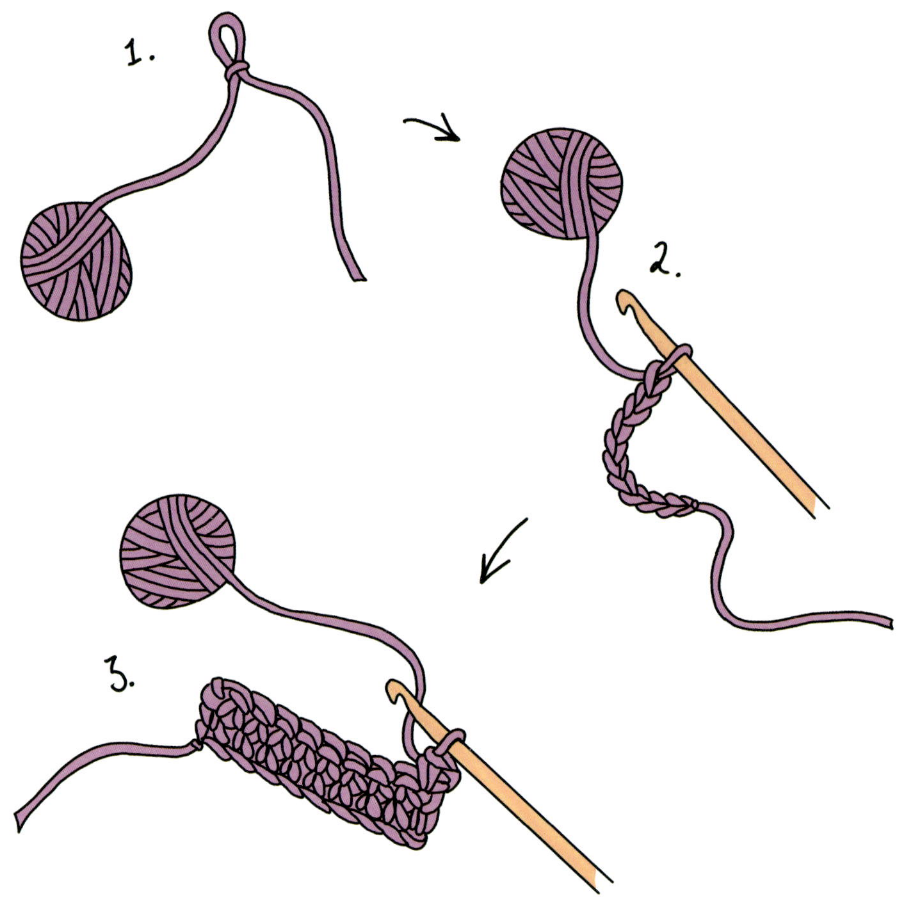

1. To begin crocheting, you will start by securing your yarn to your hook with a slip knot (tutorial on page 10).

2. Once the slip knot is complete and on your hook, you can create a chain, which will be the foundation of your crochet stitches (tutorial on page 12).

3. Then you can get started with your first crochet stitch, single crochet (tutorial on page 16).

So without further ado, let's do it!

Usually, to start crocheting, you need to create a chain. This means making some loops, which are pulled through other loops to form . . . you guessed it, a chain!

But before you start looping, how to hold your tool? There's one main method of holding your hook and yarn: yarn in one hand and hook in the other. If you're right-handed, you will hold your hook in your right hand and tension your yarn in your left. If you're left-handed, it's vice versa. Some people hold their hook like a pencil and others more like a knife. There is no right or wrong way to crochet as long as the end result comes out OK. If you're already a knitter and you knit Continental style—i.e., "picking" with the yarn held in your left hand—then this yarn and tool setup might be familiar to you. But if it's not, we promise that all the muscle memory needs is a little time and practice.

how to hold your hook

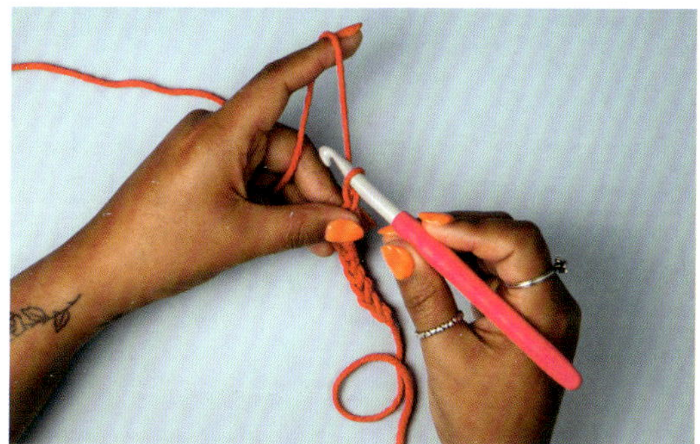

Pencil Hold

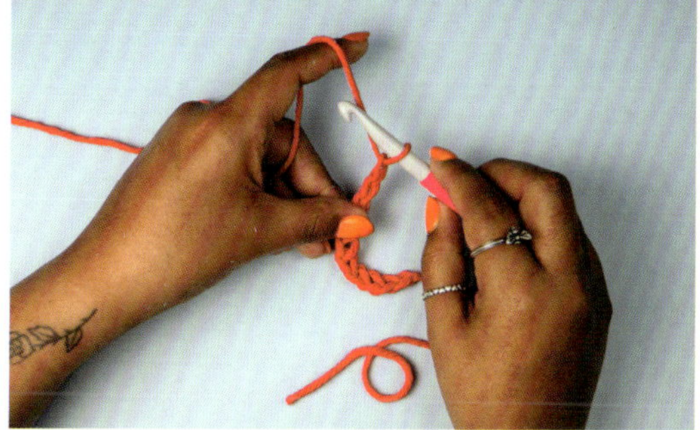

Knife Hold

how to hold your yarn

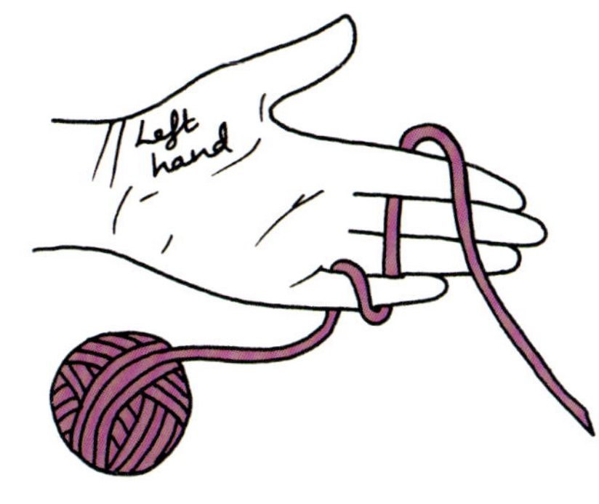

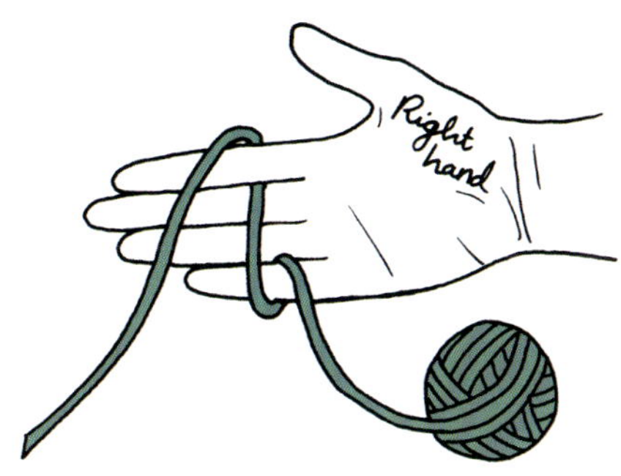

how to make a slip knot*

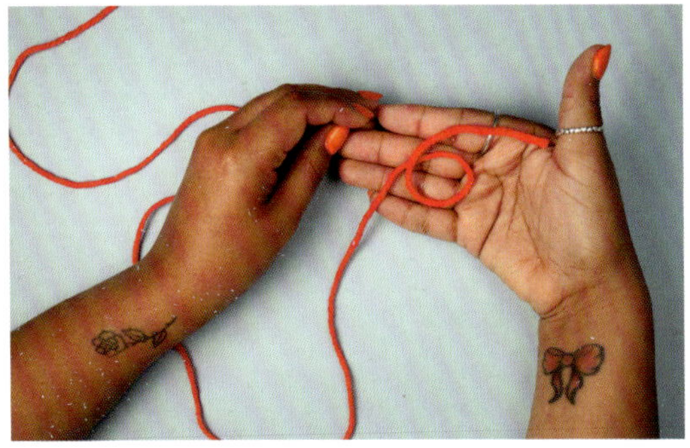

1. Cross your yarn over itself to make a loop, leaving a tail of around 15 cm/6".

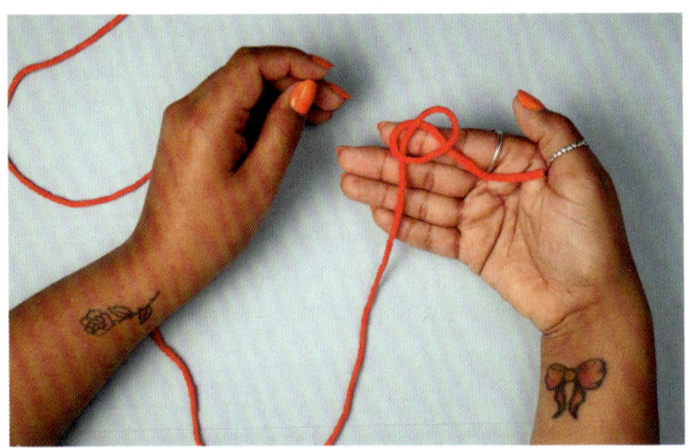

2. Cross the tail so it sits behind the loop.

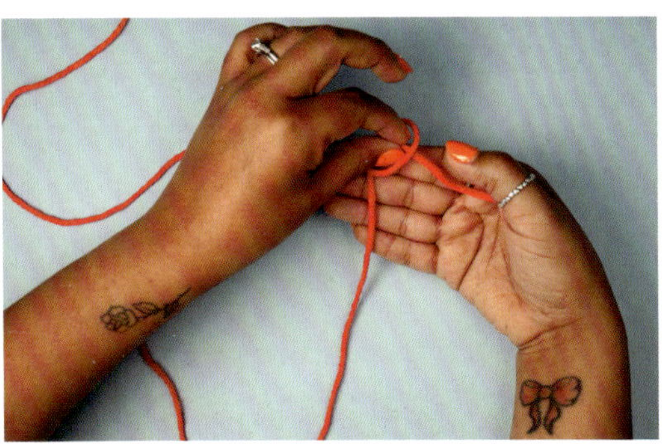

3. Pull the tail through the loop, but do not pull it all the way through.

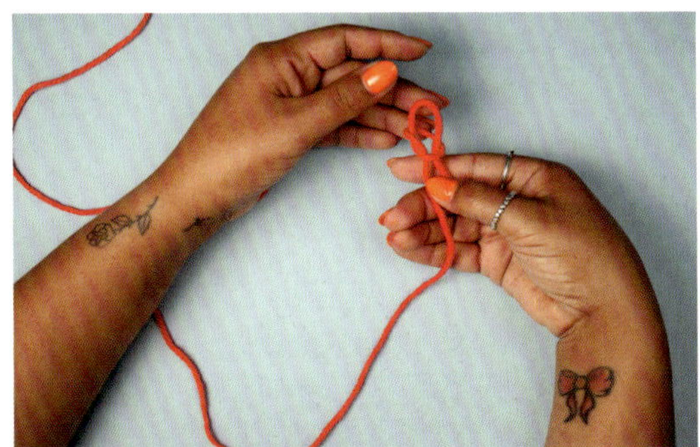

4. Your yarn should look like this.

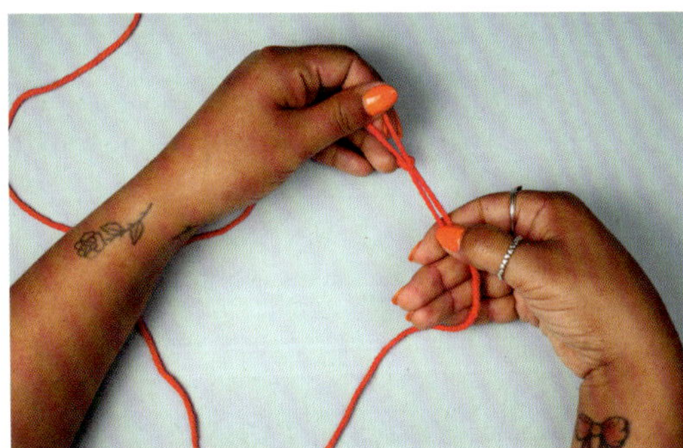

5. Pull the length of yarn attached to the ball (not the tail) to tighten. Don't pull it too hard! You want it to be firm but not too tight.

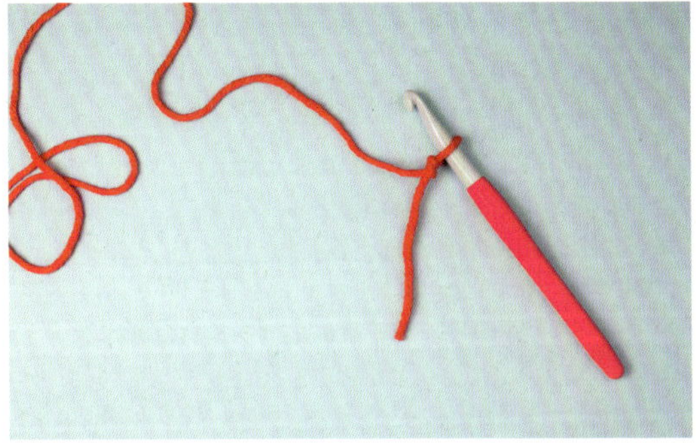

6. Your slip knot is complete. Place the loop on your hook, gently pulling the tail if necessary to make the loop smaller and ensure it fits snugly.

*For added clarity, this technique is shown in both illustrations and photos.

how to make a slip knot

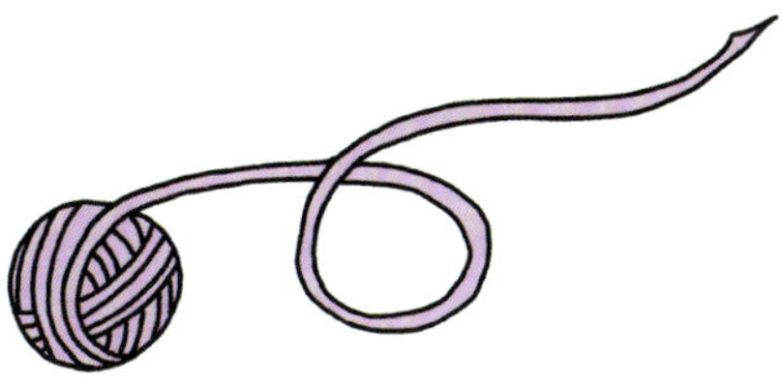

1. Cross your yarn over itself to make a loop, leaving a tail of around 15 cm/6".

2. Cross the tail so it sits behind the loop.

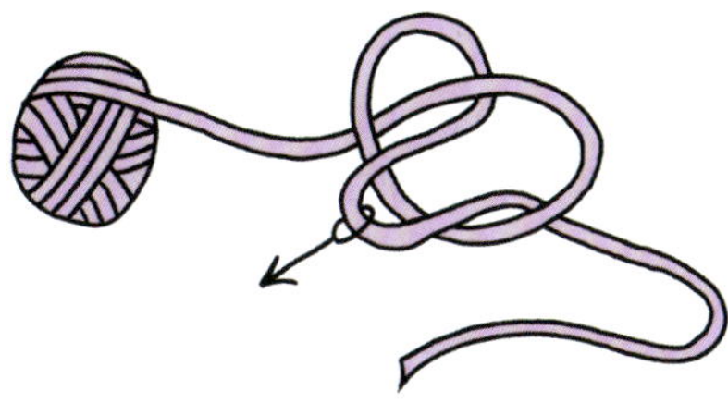

3. Pull the tail through the loop, but do not pull it all the way through.

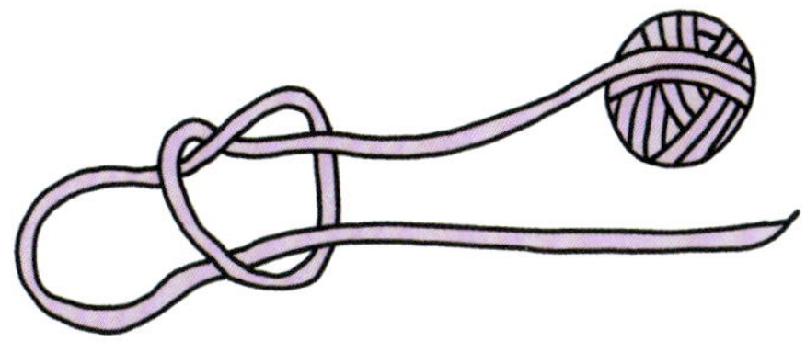

4. Your yarn should look like this.

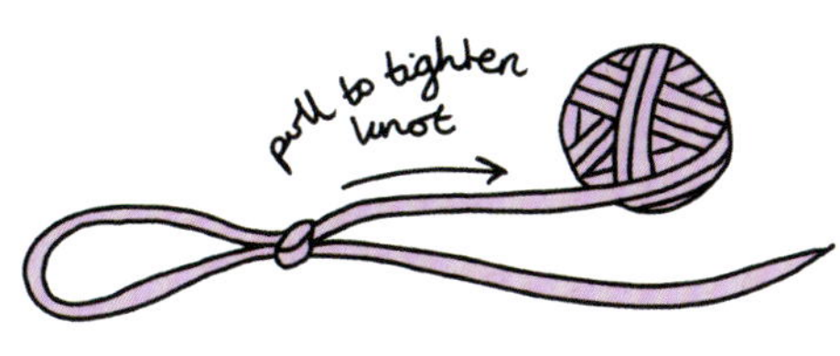

5. Pull the length of yarn attached to the ball (not the tail) to tighten. Don't pull it too hard! You want it to be firm but not too tight.

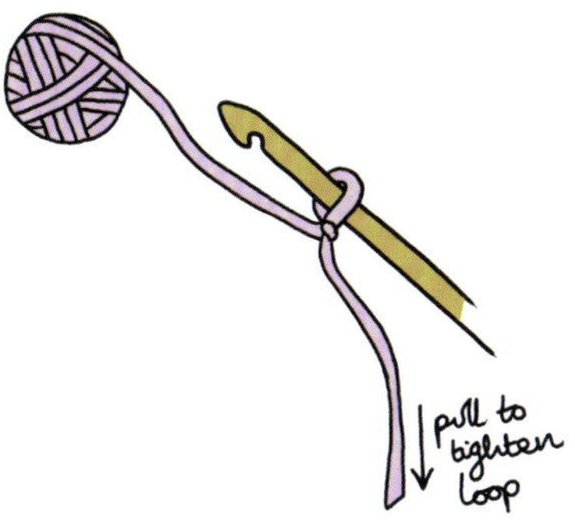

6. Your slip knot is complete. Place the loop on your hook, gently pulling the tail if necessary to make the loop smaller and ensure it fits snugly.

how to create a chain*

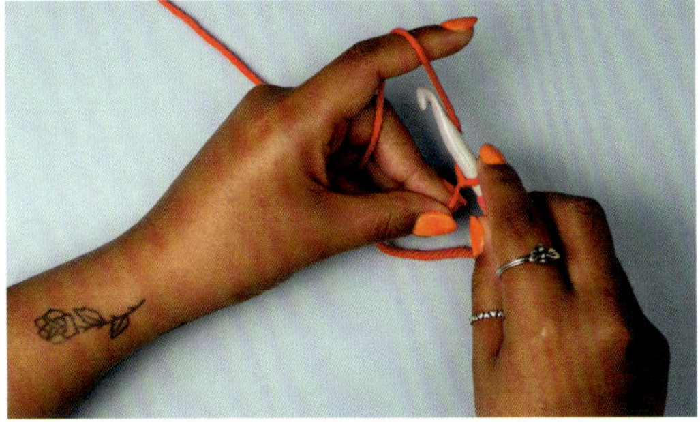

1. Make a slip knot and place it on your hook. Hold the hook with the slip knot in your dominant hand. Thread the working yarn (the part of the yarn that comes from the ball) around the index finger of the opposite hand, pulling gently to create tension. Grasp the tail end of the yarn with your thumb and middle finger to steady the slip knot.

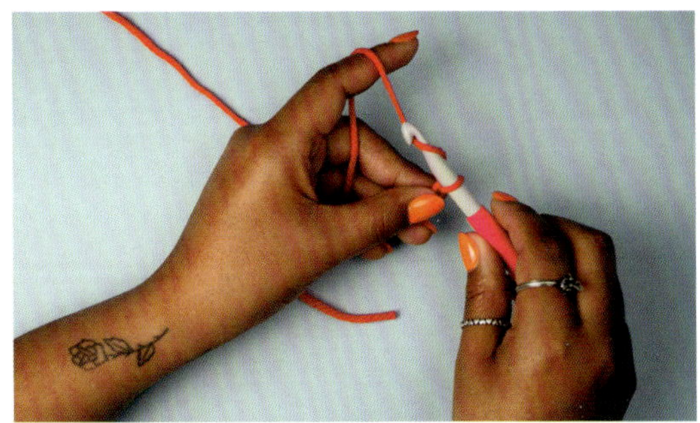

2. Move your hook under the strand of yarn and catch that strand with your hook. The yarn is now wrapped over the hook from back to front. This is called a *yarn over.*

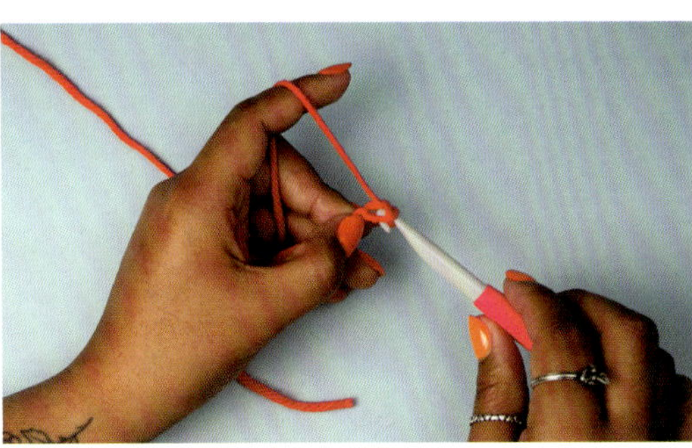

3. With the yarn caught in the hook, pull it through the original loop on the hook. Do this gently so your chains aren't too tight; remember you need to be able to get your hook into them when you start your crochet stitches.

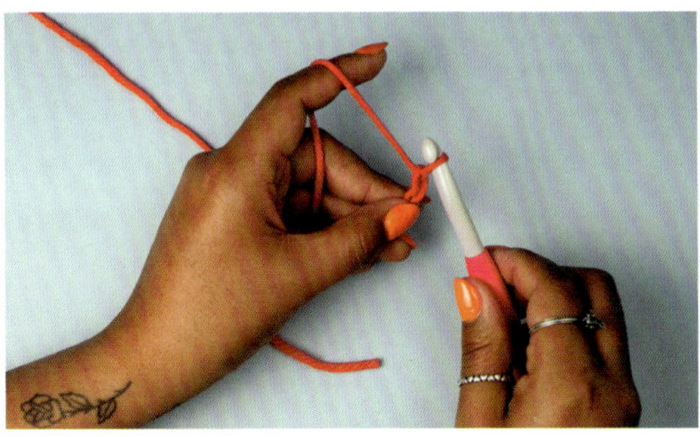

4. Once the yarn is pulled through, you will have created one chain. You should still have just one loop on your hook.

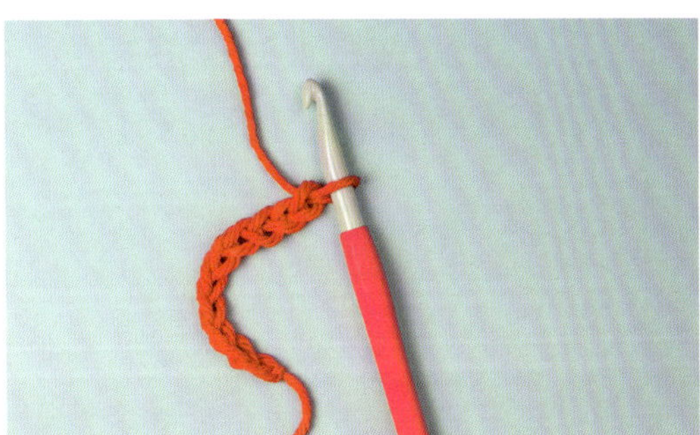

5. Repeat steps 2–4 for each chain you need (this photo shows 10). These will become the base for your first row of stitches. You will be working into the chain to make your first row.

top tip!

When making your new chains check that your chain goes onto the thicker part of your hook. That's the part that will set the size of your chain.

*For added clarity, this technique is shown in both illustrations and photos.

how to create a chain

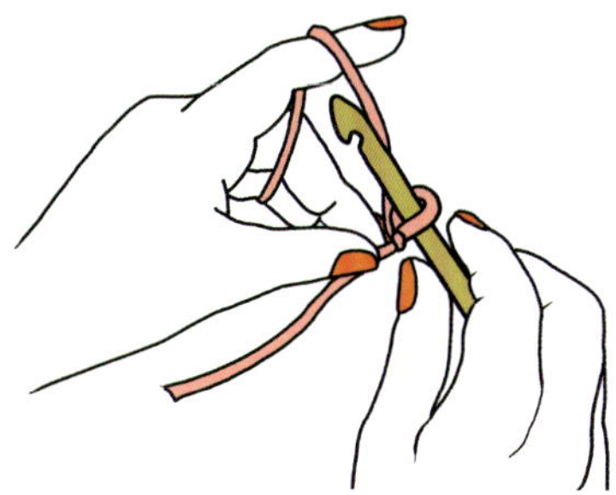

1. Make a slip knot and place it on your hook. Hold the hook with the slip knot in your dominant hand. Thread the working yarn (the part of the yarn that comes from the ball) around the index finger of the opposite hand, pulling gently to create tension. Grasp the tail end of the yarn with your thumb and middle finger to steady the slip knot.

2. Move your hook under the strand of yarn and catch that strand with your hook. The yarn is now wrapped over the hook from back to front. This is called a *yarn over.*

3. With the yarn caught in the hook, pull it through the original loop on the hook. Do this gently so your chains aren't too tight; remember you need to be able to get your hook into them when you start your crochet stitches.

4. Once the yarn is pulled through, you will have created one chain. You should still have just one loop on your hook.

5. Repeat steps 2–4 for each chain you need (this photo shows 4). These will become the base for your first row of stitches. You will be working into the chain to make your first row.

top tip!

It's worth spending some extra time practicing making chains; everything you will crochet evolves from this series of movements so it's a good idea to get some muscle memory and familiarity before you move on!

how to count chain stiches

Once you have completed your chain, you might want to check how many chain stitches you made. Did you make the right number? Let's find out! Here's a simple guide to doing just that.

Each little "V" of your chain is a chain stitch. So, when you need to check how many stitches you have made, just count them as shown here. Note that the loop on the hook isn't counted as a stitch.

lefties, don't feel left out!

If you're left-handed, you might feel left out of all the crochet content out there. Most videos, drawings, and instructions are made with only righties in mind. Meghan is a leftie and feels your pain! Unlike with knitting, which uses both hands pretty equally, we DO recommend that you crochet specifically as a left-hander. The good news: Below is a download code where you can get all the drawings and tutorials in this book flipped so that they make sense to lefties. Our other best advice? Just follow patterns as they are written. Usually, you won't need to make any changes—the pattern will just work left to right, rather than right to left. This is true for all the patterns in this book.

download code: t23lkq2c

SINGLE CROCHET

Once you have made your chain, you can start your first row of crochet stitches. How exciting! The first stitch we are going to introduce is called single crochet. Basically, you will now work back along the chain you created, and in each link of the chain, you will add a few loops. As we said, each of the basic crochet stitches involves pulling new loops through a number of loops on your hook, nothing too scary. For single crochet, you are going to insert your hook into the chain and pull through a loop. Since you already had one loop on your hook, you will now have two. You will then wrap the yarn round your hook again and pull this through those two loops. That's it!

how to insert your hook into a chain

1. You have made your chain and you're now ready to start making stitches using it as a base. Here you can see the path your hook will follow to enter the chain. You will see that you insert the hook into the second chain from your hook. This is because you are skipping your turning chain. See page 51 for more on this but for now just trust us!

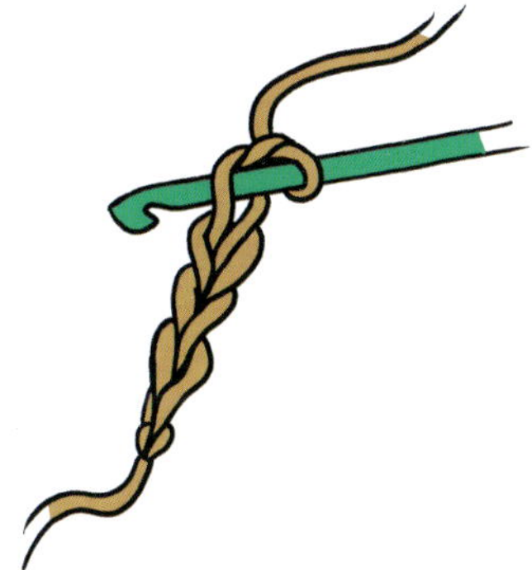

2. The hook has been inserted into the chain.

how to single crochet into a chain

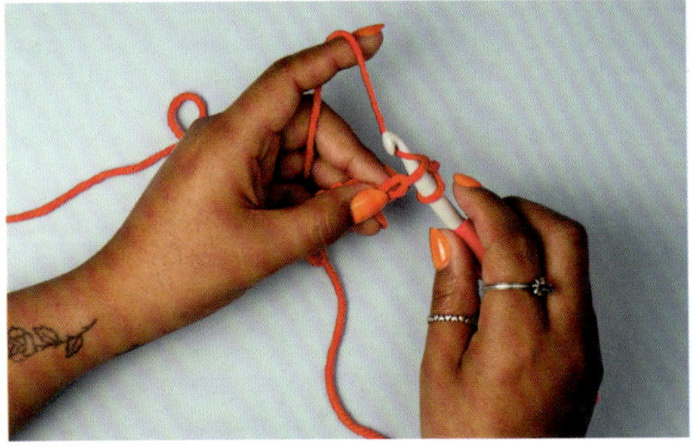

1. Once you have inserted your hook into the chain (skipping the first chain), move your hook under the working yarn and catch the strand (yarn over).

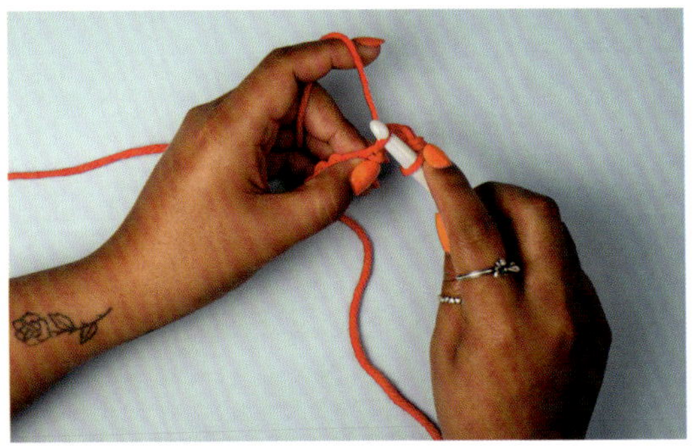

2. With the yarn caught in the hook, pull it through one loop on your hook.

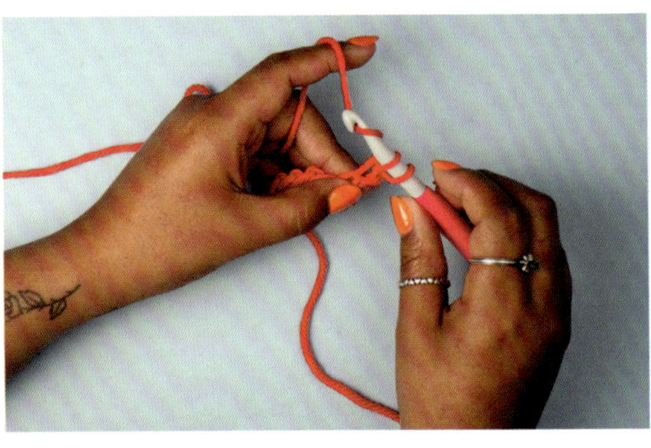

3. With two loops now on the hook, yarn over once more.

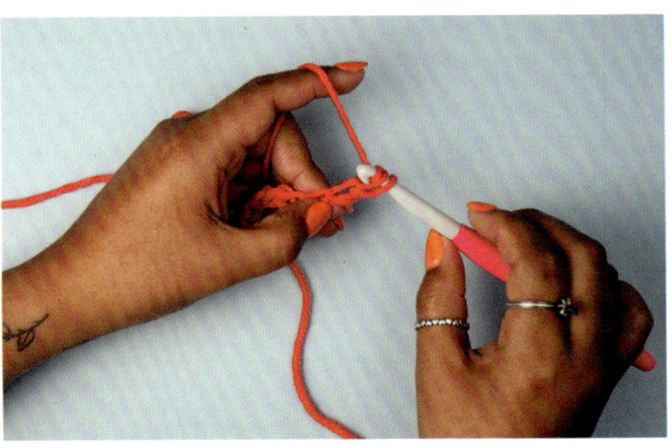

4. Pull through the two loops on the hook.

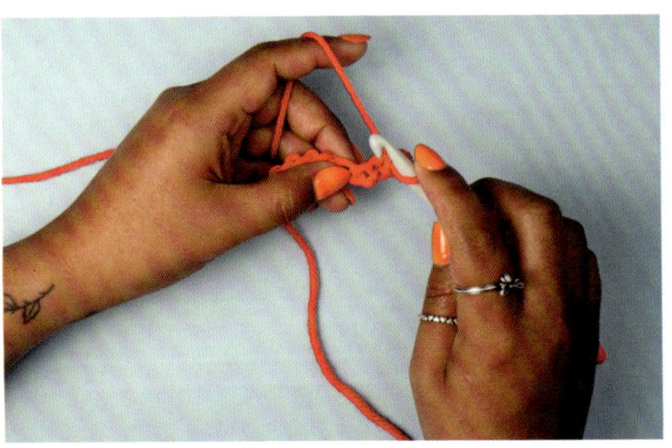

5. You will now have just one loop on your hook.

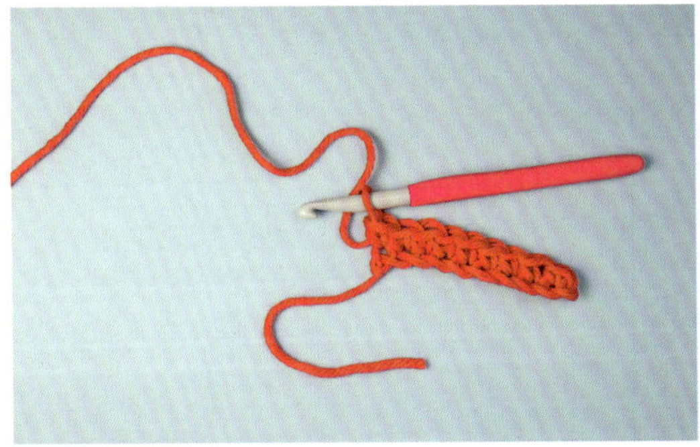

6. Work as above across each chain until they are all complete. Typically, you will then turn your work so that you can go back across those completed stitches to make the next row.

To practice and really make sure you've got the hang of it,* we recommend that you chain about 21 stitches. The final chain stitch is a *turning chain* (see below for more on this), so you will actually have 20 stitches + 1 for the turning chain in total. Then, skipping that first chain (so working into the second chain from the hook), work single crochet stitches from right to left if you're right-handed (or the opposite if you're left-handed) in every stitch until the end of the chain. Suddenly your hook will be at the left of your chain instead of at the right. (Vice versa for lefties.) You will now need to start a new row, which means you'll crochet back along the same length of stitches again. To do this you'll need to flip your work so you're looking at the other side of it. When it's time to do this in a pattern you'll see the instruction "turn."

When you start a new row, you will need to make a turning chain. The turning chain is a set number of chains at the beginning of a row that adds the height needed for the new set of stitches in that row. For single crochet (as we noted above), you just need one chain for your turning chain, then you can get on with working single crochets on top of the ones you made in the previous row.

However, you may notice that now you are working into the tops of those stitches rather than into a chain, so it all looks a little different. Have a look at the tops of the stitches you have made, and you will see that it looks like another sort of chain. A bit sturdier and better defined, but not dissimilar to the chain you started with. In terms of working your stitches, nothing is different, but you will now be inserting your hook under both sides of the V of the stitch, instead of just one.

***Warning:** This may take some time. Don't worry, just set yourself up with your favorite album or podcast, and maybe a cup of tea, and enjoy not looking at a screen for a while.

how to work into the top of a stitch

This drawing will give you a closer look at how to insert your hook into the top of the stitch in the row you just made, and how to pull a loop through, which is the starting step for your single crochet stitches.

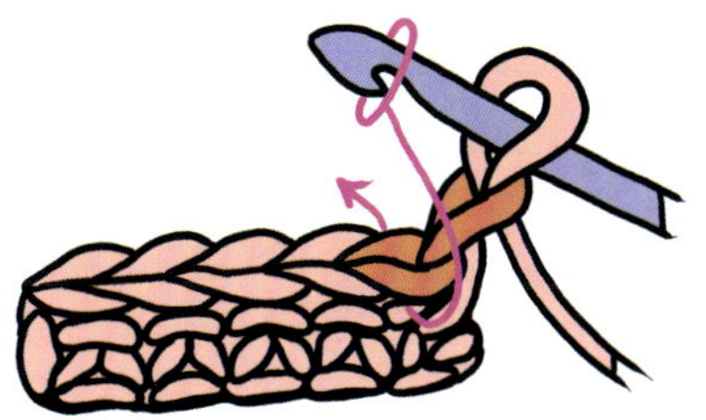

1. The first row of single crochet stitches has been completed, and you have turned and worked one chain stitch (your turning chain). The darker stitches show the first stitch in the row and the turning chain. Insert your hook into the first stitch, as shown by the arrow.

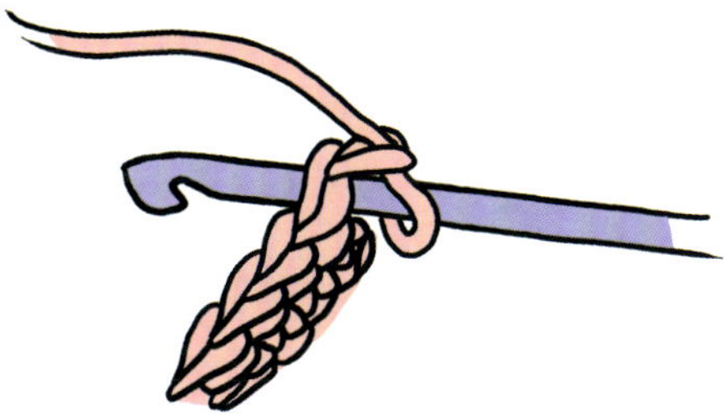

2. Insert your hook under both loops of the stitch as shown. You should be able to see both loops on top of your hook.

how to single crochet into a row of single crochet stitches

1. To work the single crochet stitch into the previous row of single crochet stitches (as opposed to working it into a chain), first work your turning chain (see page 51). For single crochet, you will work just one chain stitch.

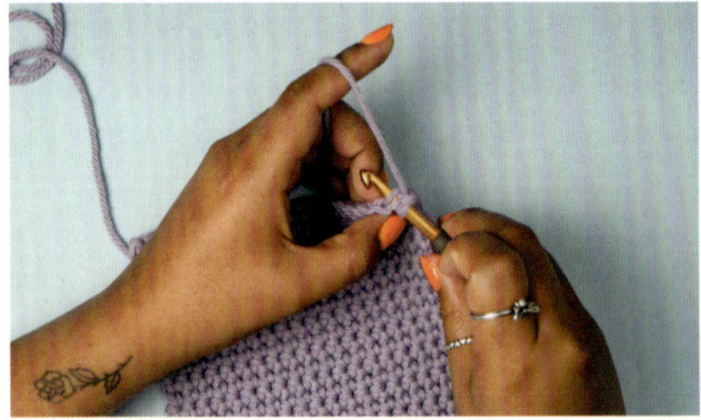

2. Insert the hook into the first stitch, under both sides of the V shape.

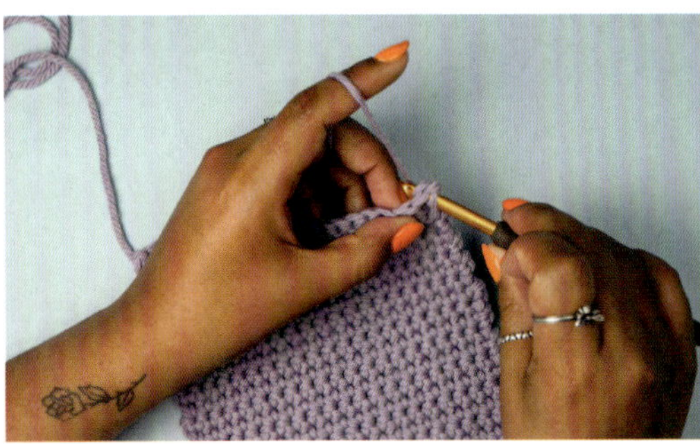

3. Yarn over (catch the yarn with your hook) and pull through the fabric from back to front.

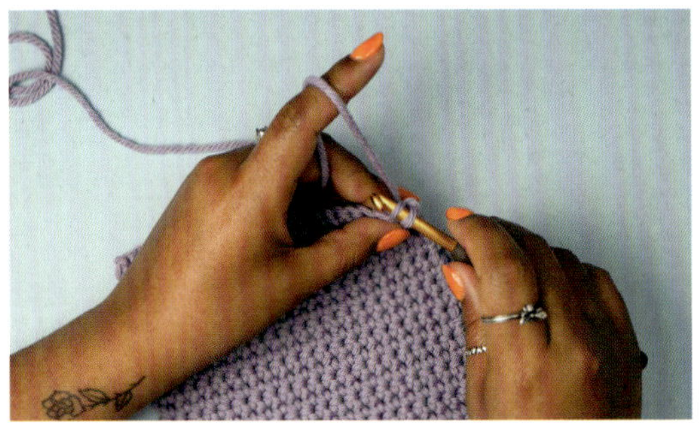

4. You will now have two loops on your hook.

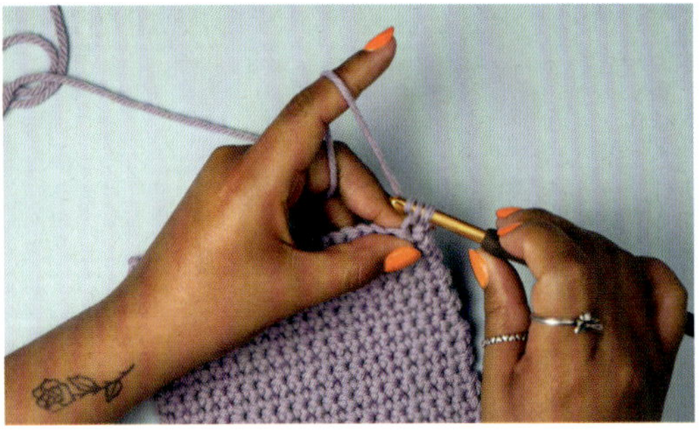

5. Yarn over once more and pull through both loops on the hook.

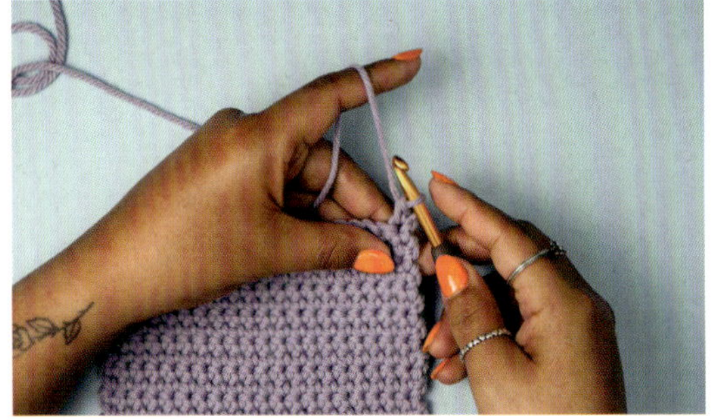

6. Your single crochet stitch is now complete. Repeat across each stitch in the row.

note: The turning chain is only necessary at the beginning of a row.

top tip!

Some people make their turning chain before they turn their work and start their next row. In this book we are turning first, then chaining, but either method works fine as long as you are consistent.

help! I have more/fewer stitches than I started with!

You may find that you end up with more or fewer stitches than you started with, and that's OK. Once you've built up some practice time, you'll get better and that will stop happening. It's also not always easy to tell which is the last stitch, and you could either accidentally make an extra stitch or turn too early. Each sideways V shape at the very top of your work is a stitch. It's worth counting your stitches before you turn your work if you aren't quite sure. (For single crochet you will not include the turning chain in your count. For all other types of stitches, you will need to include the turning chain.)

all the steps for making a crochet fabric

When you combine all the steps we've covered so far, you're making flat crochet fabric! Here's a breakdown of how all those steps work together:

1. Make a chain.
2. Work stitches into that chain.
3. Turn your work.
4. Work a turning chain.
5. Work another row.

Continue, using steps 3-5.

FASTENING OFF

When it is time to finish crocheting, you need to secure your final stitch. You only have one live stitch, so all you need to do is secure that one to secure all the previous ones.

how to fasten off

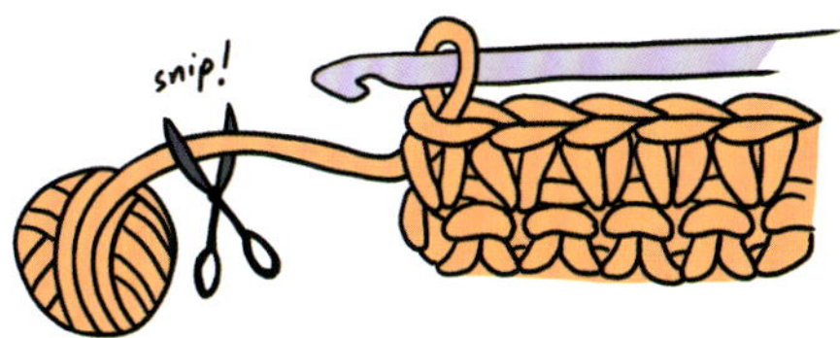

1. Keeping your stitch on your hook, cut your yarn, leaving a tail long enough to weave in. We recommend one about 15 cm/6".

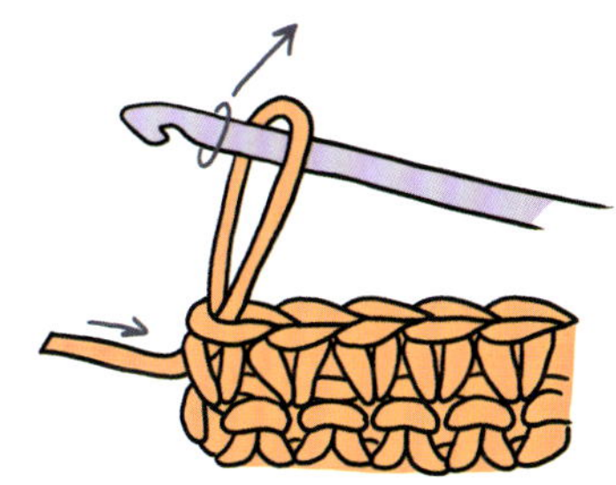

2. Now pull the yarn up through the last stitch as shown, until the end comes through.

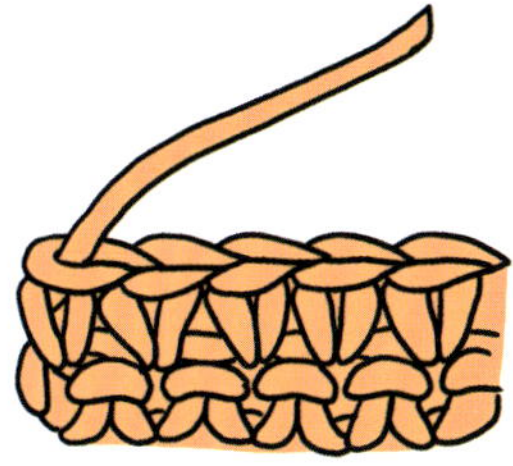

3. You've fastened off. Hurrah!

YOUR FIRST PROJECT:
single crochet coasters
(or blanket squares, or a future scarf, or . . .)

Now you're ready to crochet some little squares. We're also going to try reading a pattern. Patterns may look intimidating but fear not—it's no more complicated than writing LOL instead of "laughing out loud." So why not just "ch" for "chain" and "sc" for "single crochet"? See? Not so intimidating after all. Let's give it a go.

you will need

- A crochet hook (we recommend US size J-10/6 mm).
- Aran yarn, 70 m/77 yards (we recommend Kremke Soul Wool The Merry Merino 70, 1 ball).

If you can't get that particular yarn, don't panic. (See page 27 for more on yarn selection.) As long as your yarn is the right thickness for your hook, and you don't have a very small hook (a little trickier to see what you're doing when you're starting out), you'll be golden, we promise.

abbreviations

ch chain
sc single crochet
rep repeat

(PS: There is a whole abbreviations list at the back of this book, on page 184, so you can always refer to it if need be.)

note on US/UK crochet terms

Much like many aspects of crochet (and knitting, as it happens), the US and UK use different terminology to name crochet stitches. In this book we use US terminology, but if you are using a British pattern, it's worth double-checking what the terms mean. Here's a handy table for you. Most of these stitches aren't ones we've covered yet, but they will make sense to you very soon.

US stitch names (used in this book)	UK stitch names
Slip stitch **(sl st)**	Slip stitch **(ss)**
Chain **(ch)**	Chain **(ch)**
Single crochet **(sc)**	Double crochet **(dc)**
Double crochet **(dc)**	Treble crochet **(tr)**
Half double crochet **(hdc)**	Half treble crochet **(htr)**
Treble crochet **(tr)**	Double treble crochet **(dtr)**

single crochet square

Ch21.

Row 1: Sc in 2nd ch from hook, sc in each ch across, turn.

Row 2: Ch1, sc in each sc across, ch1, turn.

Rep Row 2 twenty more times.

Next Row: Ch1, sc in each sc across.

Fasten off. (If you need a reminder on how to fasten off, see the tutorial on page 19.)

These squares are like crocheted building blocks. You can use them on their own as coasters or sew them together to make a quilt or even a scarf.
Use a special sewing needle, called a tapestry needle, which has a blunt tip and large eye big enough to thread yarn through. On the following pages are two methods of sewing your squares together. Which you choose is totally up to you. The slip stitch seam is a bit bulkier than mattress stitch but is quicker to work. Need to seam granny squares? See page 76.

how to make a slip stitch

Slip stitches are extremely handy! They are very versatile and get used for all sorts of things (as you'll see in the course of this book). Here we are going to use them to seam two pieces of fabric together. But before we do, we thought we'd show you how to work a slip stitch, which is basically a chain stitch that you work into a stitch or through another piece of fabric, as you will see!

1. You're ready to work a slip stitch into the next stitch, highlighted in blue.

2. Insert your hook under both parts of the V of the stitch and yarn over.

3. Pull your yarn over back through the stitch. You now have two loops on your hook; the yarn over you just pulled through (shown in blue) and the stitch (pink). Pull the new loop through the stitch.

4. Ta-da! A brand-new slip stitch.

how to seam squares: slip stitch seam

1. With the wrong sides facing up, insert the hook through both pieces of fabric at adjoining sides, being sure to go through at the same rows and under two strands of yarn at each edge.

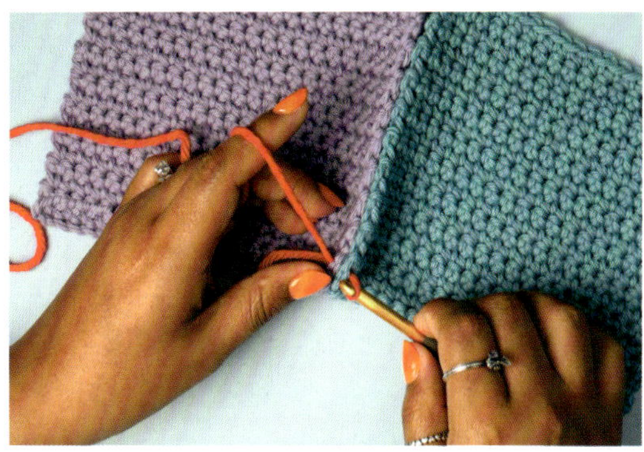

2. Attach a slip knot to the hook and draw the slip knot through both pieces of fabric (here we're using a contrast color to make it clear).

3. Insert the hook as before into the next row of stitches.

4. Yarn over and pull through again.

5. Continue as established, working evenly along the edge.

6. Cut the yarn, leaving a long tail. Yarn over and draw the tail through the last stitch to fasten off.

how to seam squares: mattress stitch

1. Thread a tapestry needle with your working yarn or a matching yarn (here we're using a contrast color to make it clear). Insert your tapestry needle into the edge of the first row of stitches on one of the pieces to be seamed, catching two strands of yarn under your needle.

2. Draw the yarn through, then insert the needle into the adjoining side of the other piece of fabric, in the same way and in the same place that you did on the first side.

3. Draw the yarn through and insert into the first side again.

4. Weave back and forth to join the two sides together, inserting the needle as before, working your way up the rows. As you continue up the rows, gently pull both ends of your yarn to close the seam at intervals, being careful not to pull too tightly and keeping the tension even. Cut the yarn, but leave a long tail to weave in so that the seam does not unravel.

TIDYING UP:
how to weave in yarn ends

You have crocheted your square and secured the final stitch. Now what? You'll notice you have yarn tails still hanging out . . . time to get those woven in.

You might be tempted to just cut the tails, or yarn ends, off your project once you're done. Eep! That could lead to your project unraveling, and we don't want that. You actually have to weave in the ends of your yarn so your stitches are nice and secure. There are about a zillion ways of doing this, but here's one of our go-to faves. See page 68 for how to weave in ends on granny squares.

1. Thread your tapestry needle with the tail. On the wrong side (back) of your work, skim the tapestry needle through a few stitch bumps.

2. Draw the needle through the stitches and pull the yarn until it's drawn completely across.

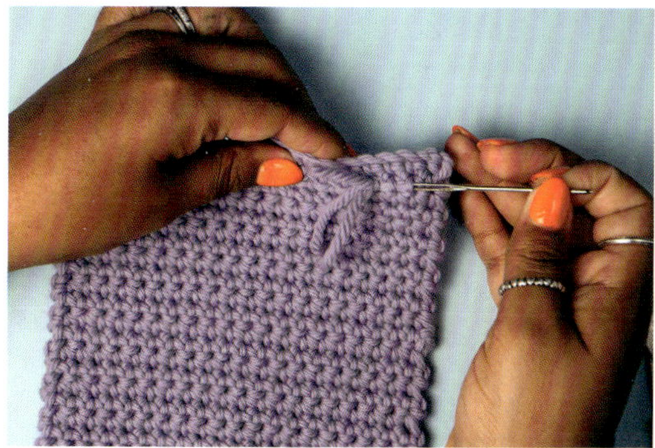

3. Repeat, working back in the opposite direction, skimming through a few stitches at a time.

4. Pull the yarn through and cut the tail close to your work, ensuring that the woven tail is hidden from the right side (front) of your fabric.

THE RIGHT STUFF:
how to choose your tools and materials

what color?

Guess what, you don't have to use the exact same yarn and hooks that your pattern (or book) calls for. In fact, the beauty and fun of crochet is that you can do it your way. The better you get, the more you can play around with your materials, but off the bat, the first place you can improvise is with color. A yarn shop will become your artist's palette. It is totally OK to spend an hour (or hours) deliberating on the perfect color for a sweater. Equally, it is totally OK to picture the perfect color in your head and then not stop until you've found the exact hand-dyed color you've been dreaming of. It probably exists. (If not, you may go down a yarn-dyeing rabbit hole yourself. We won't judge.)

which yarn?

You may also find that your local yarn shop (LYS) doesn't carry the exact yarn your pattern calls for. This is OK and not surprising. These days, there is an abundance of yarn brands, and this is to be celebrated. The fact that your pattern may have come from a designer online who lives in another country may also affect the availability of the yarn used. If you have a friendly, helpful LYS, they should be happy to guide you through choosing an appropriate substitute yarn. We both used to work in an LYS, and it was definitely part of our job to help customers in this way, so don't be shy.

If the shop is busy, or they are unable to help you, the best way to find a substitute for a yarn is to check how many meters per gram (or yards per ounce) there are in the ball of yarn (all this info will be on the yarn's label). We suggest Kremke Soul Wool The Merry Merino 70 for our Single Crochet Squares. It has 70 meters/77 yards in a 50-gram/1.75-ounce ball. If you find another yarn with a similar meterage or yardage per weight, you're golden. For example, a yarn that's 100 grams/3.5 ounces with 140 meters/153 yards would work perfectly, because it's the same ratio of meters to grams.

what if I don't like wool?

Now let's talk about fiber. Cotton is probably the most commonly used fiber for crochet, but we recommend wool for a first project. There is a time and a place for acrylics, cottons, linens, and all other fibers out there, but when it comes to starting out, we're big wool fans for a few reasons. Mainly, wool (from sheep) has great elasticity. We've found that beginning crocheters tend to work their stitches really tightly. This will ease up over time once you relax into things, but to make it easier on yourself, choosing a nice, bouncy wool will allow for some give in your crochet. Other wool pros include the fact that it's a wonderful, natural resource and can feel great in your hands. Crochet is a tactile experience that can take you away from screens and technology, so we encourage you to feel all the feels. The softness of wool varies depending on the breed of the sheep and the ways in which it has been processed, so find a wool that feels great to you.

which hook?

In terms of hooks, we recommend one with a comfy, ergonomic handle to get you started. Traditional crochet hooks are quite thin and we find these can be hard on hands, so we are great fans of the ergonomic ones. We find plastic ones can be a little sticky, so wood or metal is probably best. But no need to be too fussy. If you have something at hand or your crochet pal has lent you a hook, then go ahead and use that.

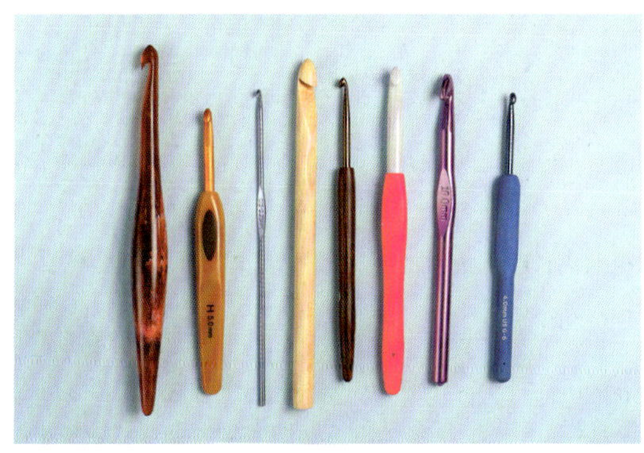

WOUND RIGHT ROUND:
wrangling skeins

Yarn comes in many forms off the shelf. Manufacturers and producers have different ways of packaging it that are good to know about up front.

1. ball

With a ball, you're ready to crochet pretty much as soon as you take the label off. You have a choice—crochet with the end of the yarn that is on the outside of the ball or dig into the middle and fish that end out. Option one is easier at the start, but option two will allow the ball to remain more stationary as you crochet, which can be nice. If you're using a hand-wound granny ball (shown in green and purple above), then you can only work from the outside, but they are so cute that we don't care!

2. bullet

Bullets are pretty much the same as balls, just a little more . . . oblong? Same deal as above with pulling the end of the yarn from the outside or inside. Fun fact: Sometimes when pulling the end of the yarn out of the inside of a ball or bullet, a clump of yarn will come out suddenly. This is what crocheters (and knitters) refer to as "yarn barf." It is the nicest barf you will ever see.

3. cake

The ball that is produced when you use a ball winder is often called a cake, and much like a regular ball, you can pull your yarn from the center or the outside. Some producers will sell their yarns already in the form of a cake. This is as useful and delicious as it sounds.

4. skein

A skein is a large loop of yarn that has been twirled around itself to form a tidy twist. Skeins are also often referred to as "hanks" of yarn. Skeins generally should not be crocheted from as is; they need to be wound into a ball or cake first. You will most often see yarn in the form of a skein when it comes from a small producer, often an independent yarn dyer. Yarn being sold in skeins means that you can see hand-dyed yarns and their subtleties, in addition to the fact that skeins lie beautifully on the shelf in yarn shops or your home.

Skeins are wound into balls using two lovely contraptions: a swift and a ball winder. They are used in tandem. The skein is stretched around the swift (the umbrella-looking thing), and then one end of the yarn is attached to the ball winder. The ball winder is either electric or powered with a hand-crank. Most local yarn shops will allow you to use their swift and ball winder or will wind your yarn for you if you've bought it there.

Here is a swift and winder setup as you might see in your LYS. Note that there are different styles of swifts; essentially, they all work the same way, holding your skein in place while you wind it. It's quick and easy to use a swift and winder (your LYS will likely be happy to show you how), but it's also possible to wind your skein by hand. Just make sure to keep the skein taut while you wind from it. It's useful to have a buddy to help with this, or if your buddies are all off doing something else (they are missing out), you can place the skein around the back of a chair, or even around your knees.

how to wind a skein by hand

1. Remove any labels from your skein and gently unwrap your yarn from a skein into a loop. To keep skeins tidy and untangled, yarn producers tie the yarn at intervals. Carefully snip these knots. One of the knots will include both ends of the skein, which makes it very easy to find.

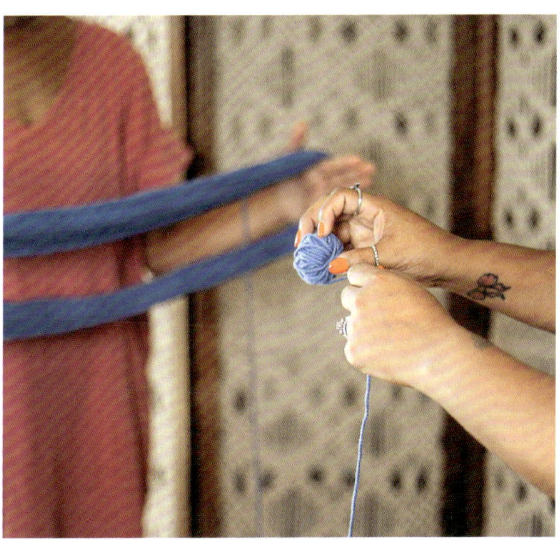

2. With the loop held neatly by another person (or around the back of a chair, or your bent knees while seated), take one end of the yarn and begin to wind the yarn into a ball (you can start by winding it around your fingers for ease, slipping it off when it feels a little sturdier). Turn the ball in your hands every so often to make an even shape. Remember not to wind too tightly! Continue until the entire skein of yarn is wound.

DOING IT RIGHT:
swatching and blocking

Those little Single Crochet Squares we did before? Those are basically swatches. What do you think of when you see the word "swatch"? Paint swatches? Fabric samples? Well, crochet swatches are essentially both. When you're about to embark on a project that needs to be a certain size, or essentially fit your body in some way, you'll want to do a *test swatch*. This means working up a small crochet sample with the yarn and hook you intend to use for your project. You see, just like how everyone has different handwriting, everyone also crochets to a different tension. Some people crochet more loosely, some more tightly than others, just because of the unique way everyone crochets. In fact, an individual might crochet differently at different times in their life—you might find you crochet more tightly when you're anxious, or more loosely when on vacation.

Every (good) crochet pattern will indicate the tension, or *gauge*, to which you should crochet. As we said, this is especially important for items that need to fit. If you crochet more loosely than the person who designed your pattern, your sweater or hat will be looser, too, sometimes to comedic effect!

To ensure that your tension is the same as the pattern's, you've got to swatch. We can't tell you how many times we've heard of a crocheter spending months on a project only to discover at the end that it doesn't fit (in fact, we've been guilty of this too). The best way to avoid this is to swatch, swatch, swatch. We'll say it again: SWATCH! Think of it as the warm-up before the big game—it'll be worth it.

how to swatch

step 1: crochet a square

So how do you swatch anyway? Check the gauge section of your pattern. It will say something like this: "15 sts & 20 rows = 10 cm/4" in single crochet." This means that 15 stitches and 20 rows should come out as a 10-cm/4" square. In order to check your gauge (to see whether you get the same number of stitches per 10-cm square as the pattern designer did), you need to have more than the number of stitches you need to measure. In this case, you will need at least 15 stitches, but we would recommend an even 20—this way, it's easier to measure and you'll get a better feel for the sort of fabric you will be making. Once you have made your starting chain, you work rows of single crochet stitches (or whatever stitch pattern is indicated) for more than 20 rows. This should result in a jaunty little square known as a swatch.

step 2: block the swatch

Now give the swatch a nice, soapy bath. This step is very important if you ever intend to wash your finished project. (Please say that you do . . .) Yarn is kind of like hair and resets when you wash it. We usually hand-wash all our crocheted items, so do the same with your swatch. Get a little wool wash, fill up a sink, and submerge the swatch. Let it soak for at least 15 minutes. When you take it out of the water, you can squeeze out the excess moisture but try not to wring it. The less you agitate your precious swatch, the better. You can roll it up in a clean towel to get some more moisture out—this will speed up the drying time. Lay the swatch out flat on an out-of-the-way surface, and once it's dry, it's time to measure it.

This process is called *blocking*. You might notice that your swatch looks better post-blocking than it did before. Getting moisture running through all your new stitches really sets them and can erase any unevenness that was there before. It's magic!

step 3: measure up

To measure the swatch, lay it out on a completely flat surface (so . . . not your lap). Grab a ruler—we like a ruler better than a measuring tape, since it's rigid and won't bend while you're measuring. You can even get a fancy gauge-measuring ruler—they're rad. Now it's time to count how many stitches you have in a 10-cm or 4" space. We do 4" instead of 1" so that there is a good sample size to get an accurate number from. Most crochet patterns will state the gauge over a space of 10 cm or 4" as well. You can use two pins to mark off the 4" length on the swatch and then count each stitch within that space, if you like. When you're counting single crochet stitches, each little tower of knots is one stitch (see How to Count Your Rows, page 53). In other stitches, each stitch might be taller or shorter, and there may even be gaps between them or other exciting patterns. But for the purposes of this swatch, we are keeping it simple.

The crocheter's jackpot is getting the correct gauge on the first try. Sometimes it happens, sometimes not, but if you don't have the same number of stitches that the pattern states off the bat, don't worry, it's completely normal—it just means you need to swatch again. You don't need to move on to a different yarn necessarily, especially if you are using the yarn called for in the pattern or something close to it. What you will need to do is change your hook size. This can be frustrating for new crocheters who don't have an arsenal of hooks (don't worry, though, one day you will). The size (circumference) of the hook essentially determines how big the loops of yarn you're making become. So, a small hook = small loops, and a big hook = big loops. That's why, typically, thinner yarns are crocheted with smaller hooks and vice versa. Say you have more stitches in 4" than are called for in your pattern. That means your stitches are smaller than they need to be, because more of them can fit into that 4" space. What you need to do is try again with a *bigger* hook. How much bigger depends on how big the discrepancy is between your gauge and the pattern's gauge, but usually one hook size up is prudent.

If you don't have enough stitches in the 4" space—i.e., fewer stitches than the pattern calls for—then you need to go down a hook size. That will make your stitches smaller, and you'll be able to fit more into that 4" space. It's also worth checking whether the yarn you are using is the right thickness. Yarn comes in a whole variety of diameters. If your yarn is too thin, it might mean you end up with too many stitches in your 4" square, and if it's too thick, you might not have enough. You can refresh your yarn knowledge on page 27. Then you swatch again. *Hopefully* the second time's a charm, but if not, guess what—time to swatch again. We find it rare that a crocheter will need to swatch more than three times, so don't let the swatching get you down. We *promise*: It. Will. Be. Worth. It.

help! I have too many stitches.
You need to try a bigger hook.

help! I don't have enough stitches.
You need to try a smaller hook.

Once you've got your stitch gauge right, check your row gauge too—i.e., how many rows of crochet stitches fit into the 10-cm/4" space vertically. Ideally, both your stitch gauge and your row gauge will be spot on, but if not, generally your stitch gauge is the more important to get right.

help! My yarn has run out. How do I join a new ball?

Don't worry, when you are getting close to finishing your first ball of yarn, it is much easier to join a new yarn than it at first appears. It's easiest to join a new color at the end of a row or round, so complete a full row or round before you are at a point where you wouldn't be able to finish the row or round with the current strand of yarn. You might be adding a new ball of yarn because you've come to the end of the old one, but there are other reasons too:

- You may find a knot in your yarn. This happens, and the best way to deal with any knot is to cut it out and rejoin your yarn.
- You may discover a thick or thin section of your yarn.
- You're changing yarn colors.

Whatever your reason, here's our how-to for joining a new yarn or color when crocheting back and forth in rows.

joining new yarn at the start of a row

1. When it comes time to join a new length of yarn, you will actually want to begin at the last stitch of the row before the one where you want to change yarn, leaving a 15 cm/6" yarn tail for weaving in.

2. When you have one step left before finishing your stitch, drop the original length of yarn and complete the last stitch with your new length of yarn.

3. Your completed stitch will end with one loop using the new length of yarn on your hook.

4. Turn and work your turning chain (here we are working three chains to start a row of double crochet stitches).

5. Continue working your row using the new length of yarn.

PART 2

THE PROJECTS

Welcome to Part 2. It's time to congratulate yourself on how far you've come already. Learning a new skill isn't always easy, but look at you! You learned how to make a chain *and* single crochet, which means you can now do what no machine can—make crocheted fabric. You're officially a crocheter.

Now that you have the basics, we'll get to some projects that will build on those stitches and really get you making things. Although it might feel challenging at times, the sense of accomplishment when you've completed a project is incredibly satisfying. The great thing about crochet is that if you make a mistake, you can unravel your yarn and begin again. Yarn is amazing that way—more often than not, your yarn will be as good as new if you feel like you need a fresh start. The key is to remember that mistakes are normal, and even the most experienced crocheters (even us) get distracted sometimes and need to redo some stitches. So be gentle with yourself, trust the process, and remember that we're here to guide you every step of the way.

Each project is designed to build on skills you've practiced in the previous ones so that you learn one or more new techniques with each pattern. We suggest working on the projects in order, but just in case you feel the urge to skip around, we've included the following handy breakdown of which techniques are introduced with each pattern for easy reference.

How Stitches Work *(page 36)*
Comparing different crochet stitches.

Project 1:
Amy/Daisy/Zahra:
Simple Cowls in Three Stitch Patterns *(page 39)*
Easy-peasy, and cozy too.

- Reading a pattern

1.1 Amy Single Crochet Cowl

- Single crochet

1.2 Daisy Double Crochet Cowl

- Double crochet

1.3 Zahra Double Crochet + Chain Cowl

- Stitch patterns incorporating chain stitches

Project 2:
Helgate Color-Block Hat *(page 55)*
A simple hat with big impact.

- Half double crochet
- Changing color
- Working different stitches in the same row

Introduction to Granny Squares *(page 62)*
Classic and clever, just like real grannies.

- Magic ring
- Working from the center out
- Working multiple stitches into one space (cluster stitches)
- Working into a chain space
- Joining rounds with slip stitches

Project 3:
Mamgu Granny Square Soap Cozy *(page 71)*
The perfect gift for friends (and you).

- Seaming granny squares using mattress stitch
- Creating a chain stitch hanging loop

Project 4:
Sophia Granny Square Blanket *(page 79)*
A lap or baby blanket for ultimate snugness.

- Even more granny practice
- Following a layout plan
- Seaming a large project

Project 5:
Sara Kerchief/Bandana *(page 85)*
Bandana, headscarf, or bow? Any way you wear it, it's cute.

- Double crochet increases
- Double crochet decreases (dc2tog) and working a short chain

Project 6:
Ashley Market Bag and Bottle Holder *(page 93)*
Infinitely useful, infinitely delightful.

- Increasing in the round
- Treble crochet
- Working a chain and rejoining it to the fabric
- Slip stitch

6.1 Market Bag
6.2 Bottle Holder

Project 7:
Salsabil Lace Top *(page 105)*
Warm weather tank, cool weather vest, loveliest first garment.

- Measuring and swatching for fit
- Working increases and decreases in pattern

Project 8:
Yly Granny Square Tee *(page 113)*
Super sweet tee that's fair and square.

- Joining granny squares as you go
- Creating a simple neckline

Project 9:
Orillia Granny-Inspired Pullover *(page 127)*
Cozy, comfy, cute.

- Joining a chain to work in the round
- Raglan increases
- Decreasing in granny stitch pattern
- Ribbing working through back loops only
- Working into both sides of a chain

Project 10:
Atwin Textured Cushion Cover *(page 141)*
Show off your skills with this intermediate stitch.

- Fancy stitches: interlocking blocks
- Working into the row below
- Working with three colors
- Picot edging

Project 11:
Quinte House Slippers *(page 153)*
WFH style never looked so good.

- Measuring feet
- 3-D shapes
- Following a chart
- Single crochet decreases

Project 12:
Kennedy Amigurumi Pincushion *(page 167)*
Crochet flower power.

- Stuffing crochet objects
- Sewing 3-D shapes together

HOW STITCHES WORK

Now that you've got single crochet under your belt, you're ready to branch out. Before we jump in, we'd like to help you understand the building blocks of basic crochet stitches. You might have noticed that the names for the main stitches are single, half double, double, treble, and double treble. While there are certainly other stitches, these are the most commonly used and are just variations of one another. The difference between them has to do with how many loops you wrap around your hook and how many times you pull those loops through each other.

The photo below shows these stitches in a row for comparison.

- Blue: single crochet
- Orange: half double crochet
- Yellow: double crochet
- Pink: treble crochet
- Green: double treble crochet

And here's each of those main stitches on their own (we omitted double treble in green as it is less common and not used in this book):

Single Crochet

Half Double Crochet

Double Crochet

Treble Crochet

Below is a comparison of these stitches in swatches to give you an idea of what kind of fabric each stitch makes:

Crochet is fascinating because you can mix these stitches to make rows of different heights, giving you a really incredible toolbox for creating different shapes and textures. You'll understand this a bit better when we get to the hat pattern in the book (see page 55), which uses stitches of different heights to create the tapered shape at the top.

As you can also see, each stitch creates a different density of fabric. Single crochet is dense and solid, and, assuming you aren't using an inordinately large hook for your yarn, it doesn't have gaps between stitches. As you move through the range of stitches and they become "taller," you can see that they create a more open fabric. You'll notice that in the slipper pattern (see page 153), for example, half double crochet is used in order to make a solid fabric, while in the market bag (see page 93), which is meant to be quite open, treble crochet is used for the mesh portion.

We'll walk you through how to make each new stitch as we get to them in the patterns that follow, but for reference, here's where you can find them:

Single crochet: see page 15
Half double crochet: see page 61
Double crochet: see page 46
Treble crochet: see page 100

project 1

AMY DAISY ZAHRA

Simple Cowls in Three Stitch Patterns

project 1:

SIMPLE COWLS IN THREE STITCH PATTERNS

These three cowls are designed to allow a beginner to work on a larger piece of fabric than a swatch but aren't so big that they will be disheartening or overwhelming. There are three options to choose from: single crochet, double crochet, and double crochet + chain (simple lace) for the more ambitious. There's also the option to twist before seaming. Even if you decide not to make each cowl, give each set of instructions a try so you can get the hang of the new stitches.

notes on construction:

The cowls are constructed by making long rectangles (like a scarf, but shorter) that are joined at the short ends to form a loop.

techniques you need to know:

- Chain (see page 12)
- Single crochet (see page 15)
- Slip stitch seaming (see page 23)

techniques introduced:

- Reading a pattern (see page 41)
- Double crochet (see page 46)
- Stitch patterns incorporating chain stitches (see Double Crochet + Chain, page 50)
- Working into a chain space (see page 50)
- Working into a turning chain (see page 52)
- Using a stitch marker (see page 52)
- Counting rows (see page 53)

note: The yarn we've suggested for this pattern is plump and round and has a high twist. By "high twist" we mean that the strands (or *plies*) that make up the yarn are twisted together tightly (most yarns are made up of more than one ply, but some are not). This is good for beginners as the yarn is less likely to split when you're working with it, meaning your hook won't get stuck inside your yarn. Rather, your yarn will glide around your hook, allowing you to create stitches smoothly and relatively easily. If you can't get your hands on the exact yarn we've suggested for this pattern, we suggest looking for or asking at your local yarn shop for another yarn with a high twist.

top tip: brackets

In the third of these three cowls, Zahra (see page 49), you will notice some pattern instructions appear in brackets [like this]. The brackets simply denote a group of stitches or instructions that will be repeated. For example, when you see [ch1, skip next st, 1dc in next st] to last st, you will repeat the instructions within the brackets until you have only one stitch left.

You'll also sometimes see longer stitch repeats indicated by asterisks. Just follow the instructions as written in the pattern and you'll be on the right track!

help! The number of chain stitches to start my project doesn't seem to add up.

We know it can be a little confusing to chain 22 stitches to cast on 20 (as you do in the Daisy crochet cowl, which uses double crochet). Since the last 3 chains are a 3-ch (the first stitch), it can seem like the numbers don't add up. But just remember that chains 20, 21, and 22 are the 3-ch turning chain that is counted as your first double crochet.

Don't forget that when working in single crochet, (usually) your turning chain doesn't count as a stitch, so you will chain 21 stitches to cast on 20, and the 21st chain is a turning chain only!

become a pattern-reading pro

Patterns can be daunting, we get it. Remember, abbreviations for stitches are no more complicated than using LOL instead of "laugh out loud," for example. Ch = chain, no biggie, right? You'll read patterns as quickly as you can type BTW, ILYSM, TTYL . . . LOL!

For this first pattern, we thought we'd give you a cheat sheet of what each abbreviation means. For future patterns, all abbreviations are listed in the back of this book, on page 184, for easy reference.

ch	chain
dc	double crochet
sc	single crochet
sp	space
st(s)	stitch(es)

pattern 1.1

AMY single crochet cowl

One size: 16.5 cm/6½" deep x 101 cm/39¾" circumference

Yarn: Manos del Uruguay Cardo (bulky weight; 100% Corriedale wool; 100 m/109 yds per 100-g/3.5-oz skein)

Shade: Spirulina; 2 skeins

OR approx 200 m/218 yds of bulky weight yarn

Gauge: 12 sts & 12 rows = 10 cm/4" in single crochet using US L-11/8mm hook, after blocking

Hook: US L-11/8 mm

Always use a hook size that will result in the correct gauge after blocking.

Notions: Tapestry needle

PATTERN

Ch21.

Set-up row: 1sc in 2nd ch from hook (missed 1-ch does not count as st), 1sc in each ch to end, turn. *20 sts*

Row 1: Ch1 (does not count as st), 1sc in each st to end, turn.

Rep Row 1 until cowl measures 101 cm/39¾" or desired length (just remember that if you make it longer, you may need more yarn).

Fasten off, leaving a tail long enough for seaming.

FINISHING

Twist the cowl once if desired (the sample shown is twisted), then seam using the slip stitch method.

a. Depth: 16.5 cm/6½"
b. Circumference: 101 cm/39¾"

pattern 1.2

DAISY double crochet cowl

One size: 16.5 cm/6½" deep x 101 cm/39¾" circumference

Yarn: Manos del Uruguay Cardo (bulky weight; 100% Corriedale wool; 100 m/109 yds per 100-g/3.5-oz skein)

Shade: Pumpkin; 2 skeins

OR approx 200 m/218 yds of bulky weight yarn

Gauge: 12 sts & 6.5 rows = 10 cm/4" in double crochet using US K-10.5/6.5 mm hook, after blocking

Hook: US K-10.5/6.5 mm

Always use a hook size that will result in the correct gauge after blocking.

Notions: Tapestry needle

PATTERN

Ch22.

Set-up row: 1dc in 4th ch from hook (missed 3-ch counts as dc), 1dc in each ch to end, turn. *20 sts*

Row 1: Ch3 (counts as first dc), 1dc in each st to end, turn.

Rep Row 1 until cowl measures 101 cm/39¾" or desired length (just remember that if you make it longer, you may need more yarn).

Fasten off, leaving a tail long enough for seaming.

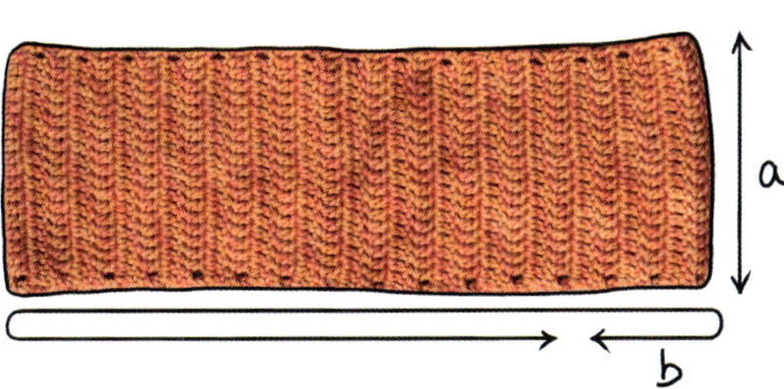

FINISHING

Twist the cowl once if desired (the sample shown is untwisted), then seam using the slip stitch method.

a. Depth: 16.5 cm/6½"

b. Circumference: 101 cm/39¾"

DOUBLE CROCHET

Double crochet can be worked into a chain or an already completed row of stitches. If working into a chain, you will put the first stitch into the fourth chain from your hook. If you have a row of stitches already completed (as pictured above), you will need a turning chain, which counts as the first stitch in the row.

help!
There's a hole after my turning chain.

Because a turning chain isn't exactly the same thing as a crochet stitch, sometimes you will see a little gap between it and the following stitches. This is nothing to worry about, but you can take a closer look and make sure you haven't skipped a stitch (see the turning chain cheat sheet on page 179 to remind yourself which stitch you should be working into after your turning chain). If you haven't, then you're doing it right.

1. (Skip this step if you are working into a chain.) If you are working into an already completed row, make your turning chain by chaining three. This counts as your first stitch in that row, so you will then skip working into the first stitch.

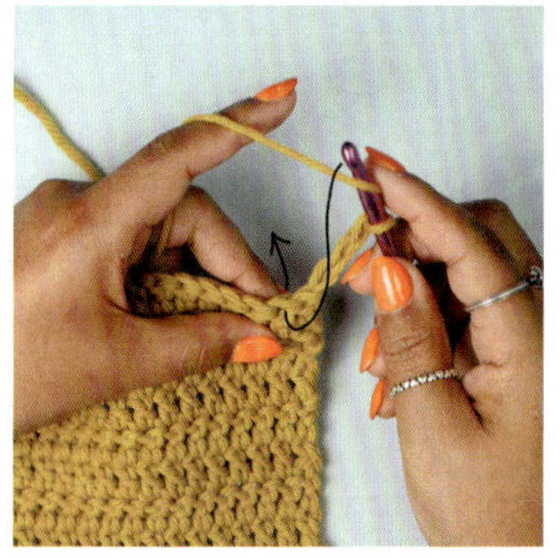

2. Yarn over (catch the yarn with your hook). You will have two loops on your hook.

3. Insert the hook into the following stitch. If working into the chain, refer to the instructions on page 15 for guidance on where to insert your hook.

4. Yarn over and pull through the fabric from back to front. You will now have three loops on your hook.

5. Yarn over again. (Four loops on the hook.)

6. Pull the yarn over you just made through the next two loops on your hook.

7. Yarn over again. (Three loops on the hook.)

8. Pull the yarn over you just made through the last two loops on your hook.

9. Your double crochet stitch is complete.

pattern 1.3

ZAHRA double crochet + chain cowl

One size: 16.5 cm/6½" deep x 101 cm/39¾" circumference

Yarn: Manos del Uruguay Cardo (bulky weight; 100% Corriedale wool; 100 m/109 yds per 100-g/ 3.5-oz skein)

Shade: Peach Blossom; 2 skeins

OR approx 200 m/218 yds of bulky weight yarn

Gauge: 12 sts & 6 rows = 10 cm/4" in pattern using US K-10.5/6.5 mm hook, after blocking

Hook: US K-10.5/6.5 mm

Always use a hook size that will result in the correct gauge after blocking.

Notions: Tapestry needle

PATTERN

Ch23.

Set-up row: 1dc in 4th ch from hook (missed 3-ch counts as dc), 1dc in each ch to end, turn. *21 sts*

Row 1: Ch3 (counts as dc), 1dc in next st, [ch1, skip next st, 1dc in next st] to last st, 1dc in last st, turn.

Row 2: Ch3 (counts as dc), 2dc in each 1-ch sp to last 2 sts, 1dc in each of last 2 sts, turn.

Rep Rows 1 and 2 until cowl measures approx 101 cm/39¾" or desired length, ending with Row 1 (just remember that if you make it longer, you may need more yarn).

Fasten off, leaving a tail long enough for seaming.

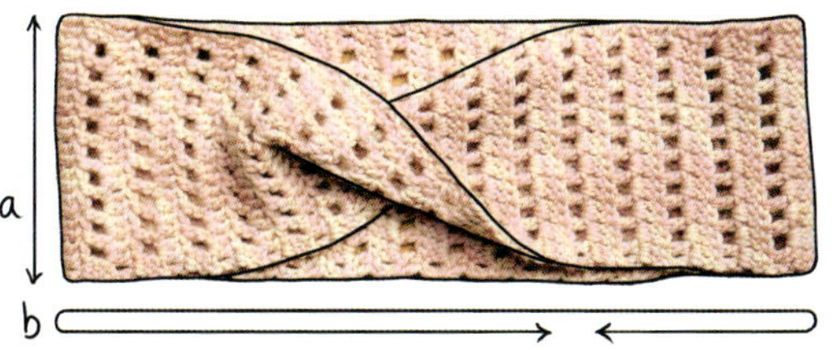

FINISHING

Twist the cowl once if desired (the sample shown is twisted), then seam using the slip stitch method.

a. Depth: 16.5 cm/6½"
b. Circumference: 101 cm/39¾"

double crochet + chain

1. This stitch pattern is created by simply alternating double crochet and chain stitches. Here we've worked some double crochet stitches, then worked one chain stitch.

2. To continue, skip the next stitch and work a double crochet stitch (as shown on page 46) into the following stitch.

3. You will now have an (intentional) hole in your row. Continue by working one chain, skipping the next stitch, and working one double crochet in the following stitch as indicated in your pattern.

working cluster stitches into a chain space

1. When working into a chain space, aka ch-sp (rather than inserting your hook into a stitch or a chain), you insert the hook into the space made by chain stitches in the previous row or round. Here you can see the hook poised for the next double crochet stitch into a chain space, with the yarn over the hook.

2. Insert your hook into the chain space.

3. Pull up a loop through the chain space as shown.

4. Complete your double crochet (or other stitch as advised in your pattern) as shown. You will see that the stitch sits around the chain.

all about turning chains

As we mentioned in Part 1, turning chains are chain stitches at the beginning of a row. The turning chain brings your new row to the correct height. Think about when you need a new line of text when you're typing on a computer. You press Enter to go to the next line and create a new level of text. Your turning chain does the same thing—it brings your hook to the next level for your new row.

The number of chains in your turning chain will depend on what stitch you're making in the new row. The taller the stitch, the more chains you'll make.

Here you can see the turning chains for single, half double, and double crochet.

- Single crochet (sc, shown in purple) requires one stitch for its turning chain
- Half double crochet (hdc, shown in red) requires two stitches for its turning chain
- Double crochet (dc, shown in yellow) requires three stitches for its turning chain

So that's how you make your turning chain to *start* your row. If you are working in any stitch other than single crochet, your turning chain will almost always count as the first stitch in your row (double-check the pattern you're working on to be sure). If your turning chain does count as a stitch, when counting the number of stitches you've made, you'll want to count that turning chain. When counted as a stitch, the turning chain starts as the first stitch in your row, but it becomes the *last* stitch to work into in the following row. Depending on your pattern instructions, you'll likely need to work *into* the turning chain from the previous row just as you have in the rest of the stitches in your row.

how to work into a turning chain

1. At the end of your row, you'll come to the turning chain from the previous row. For taller stitches like double or treble crochet (pictured here), it should be a lot more obvious where the turning chain is compared to single crochet.

2. Here you can see quite clearly the V of the top of the turning chain where you will need to insert your hook. Work a stitch into the chain to complete the row. This works the same way any time you need to work into the top of a turning chain, regardless of the height of that chain.

using a stitch marker to indicate a turning chain

If you're still worried about not being able to see where your turning chain is when you come back to it on the following row, use a locking stitch marker to easily indicate where the turning chain is located. As soon as you complete the turning chain and the following stitch in the row, place a locking stitch marker into the top of the turning chain. When you return to it on the following row, you will be able to see where that chain is clearly thanks to the marker. Remove the marker and work into the turning chain as instructed.

how to count your rows

Now that you've worked several rows you might be wondering how you keep track of them! You can use a row counter to keep track (see page 106) but it's also useful to be able to "read" your stitches.

Here are two illustrations to help guide you on your journey to stitch literacy. You can see four rows of single crochet and four rows of double crochet with the arrows indicating which direction the row has been worked. Both drawings show five stitches across. You might notice alternate rows look different—that's because the front and back of the stitches look different.

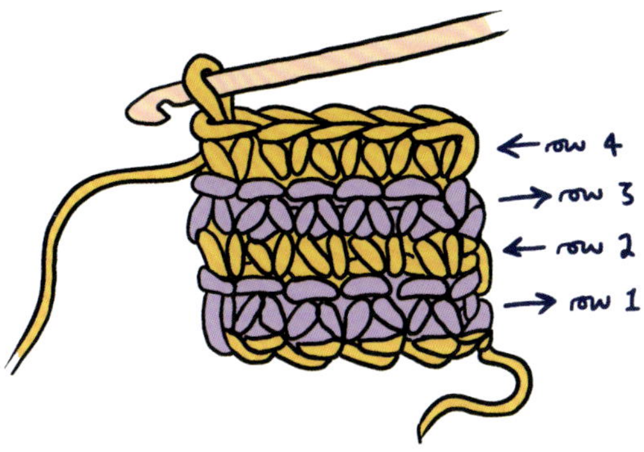

single crochet

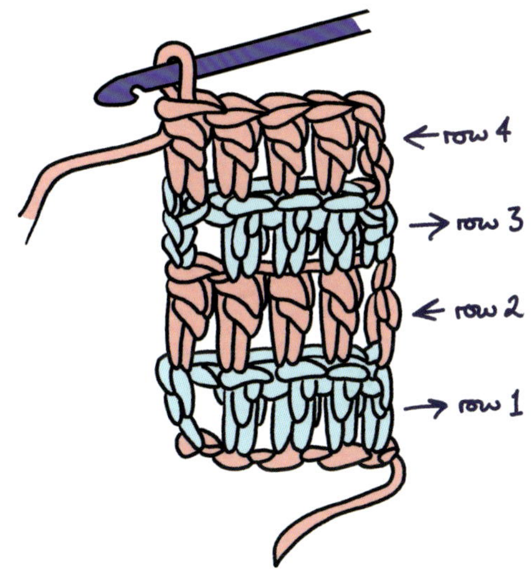

double crochet

project 2

HELGATE

Color-Block Hat

project 2:
COLOR-BLOCK HAT

This hat is worked sideways and flat, seamed lengthwise, and then the top is drawn closed. Shorter stitches are worked at the top so that the top of the hat has a smaller circumference. This means that you get to see the magic of the different heights of crochet stitches in an easy and quick project. Our samples are all worked in two colors, but of course more colors, or a single color, are also an option. We love the graphic possibilities of the vertical color change that this construction allows. You will use double crochet, single crochet, and a new stitch, half double crochet, in this project.

notes on construction:
Helgate is crocheted sideways using the varied heights of stitches to make the width of the crown narrower than the width of the brim. When measuring how long the piece is, measure the brim (the longer side).

techniques you need to know:
- Chain (see page 12)
- Single crochet (see page 15)
- Double crochet (see page 46)
- Slip stitch seaming (see page 23)

techniques introduced:
- Half double crochet (see page 61)
- Changing color (see page 33)
- Working different stitches in the same row

note: The word *ease* in crochet patterns refers to how tight or loose an item will be relative to the part of the body it's intended for. If something has *positive ease*, it means the final item will be bigger than your body part (as in an oversized sweater), and if it has *negative ease*, it means it will be a bit smaller than your body part. With hats, you want them to be a bit snug so they don't fall down around your eyes; therefore, they have negative ease. Luckily, the yarn and the stitch pattern used in this hat both have stretch, so the slight negative ease included in this pattern means your finished hat should be both comfortable and well-fitting. That is, as long as you took the time to swatch!

top tip: right side vs. wrong side

In this pattern, we'll introduce you to the world of *right side* and *wrong side* (RS and WS). The phrase "right side" refers to the side of your crocheted fabric that will face out, like the outside of a sweater, or in the case of this pattern, a hat. Sometimes it can be difficult for beginners to discern which is which while making something, so we suggest using a stitch marker to mark the right side of your work as soon as you complete the first row. You can move the marker up as you go so it remains easy to see.

top tip: adding a new color

We love how easy it is to make this hat using two colors. We introduced you to adding a new ball of yarn in Part 1 (see page 33) and changing to a new color is no different. Want your hat to be all one color? Just ignore the part of the pattern where it says "Change to Yarn B." The beauty of making your own things is that you get to decide.

finishing your hat

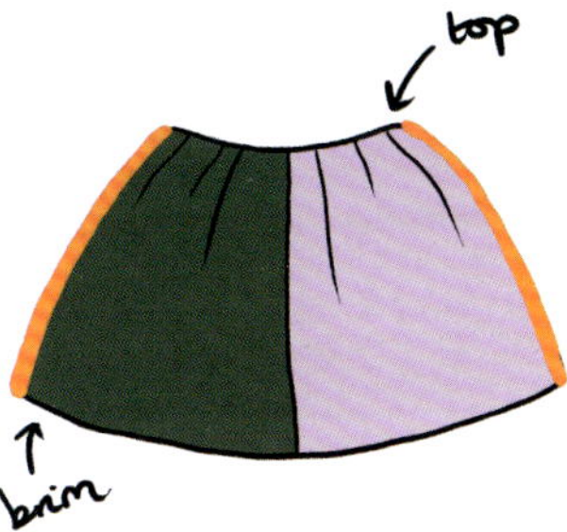

When you finish crocheting your hat, you will have a piece of fabric that looks like this. The top is the shorter side. Fold the hat in half with right sides together and seam the sides highlighted in orange.

Using a tapestry needle, thread your yarn in and out of the circumference of the top and pull tight to gather. Then weave in your ends.

Turn the hat inside out so the seam is on the inside. Fold your brim up and you have a hat!

pattern 2

HELGATE color-block hat

Sizes: 1 (2, 3, 4)

To fit head circumference: 50 (53, 56, 58.5) cm/ 19¾ (20¾, 22, 23)", to be worn with approx 2.5–5 cm/1–2" negative ease

Finished dimensions: 46 (48, 51, 53) cm/ 18 (19, 20, 20¾)" brim circumference x 19 cm/ 7½" long (with brim folded)

Yarn: Kelbourne Germantown Bulky (bulky weight; 100% North American wool; 112 m/123 yds per 100-g/3.5-oz ball)

Shades:

Yarn A: Pink; 1 ball **Yarn B:** Honey; 1 ball

OR

Yarn A: Forest Green; 1 ball **Yarn B:** Lilac; 1 ball

OR

Yarn A: Emerald; 1 ball **Yarn B:** Jade; 1 ball

OR approx:

Yarn A: 70 (75, 79, 84) m/77 (82, 86, 92) yds of bulky weight yarn

Yarn B: 70 (75, 79, 84) m/77 (82, 86, 92) yds of bulky weight yarn

Gauge: 12 sts & 6.5 rows = 10 cm/4" in double crochet using US J-10/6 mm hook, after blocking

Hook: US J-10/6 mm

Always use a hook size that will result in the correct gauge after blocking.

Notions: Tapestry needle, locking stitch marker

top tip: parentheses

Most patterns include multiple sizes, providing different instructions for each size. Sizes are organized in a parenthetical list and instructions follow the same sequence throughout. So if we knit size 2 of our hat from the size list 1 (2, 3), we follow the second number throughout the pattern.

PATTERN

Using Yarn A, ch34.

Set-up row: 1dc in 4th ch from hook (missed 3-ch counts as dc), 1dc in each st to end, turn. *32 sts*

Row 1 (WS): Ch3 (counts as first dc throughout), 1dc in each st to last 5 sts, 3hdc, 2sc, turn.

Row 2 (RS): Ch1, 1sc, 3hdc, 1dc in each st to end, turn.

note: Place a locking stitch marker to identify the RS of the fabric.

Repeat Rows 1 and 2 until piece measures 23 (24, 25.5, 26.5) cm/9 (9½, 10, 10½)" (approx 15 [16, 17, 18] rows in total), ending with Row 1.

Change to Yarn B. Work Row 2, then rep Rows 1 and 2 until piece measures 23 (24, 25.5, 26.5) cm/ 9 (9½, 10, 10½)" from color change, ending with Row 1.

Fasten off.

top tip: where to make your stitches

Sometimes pattern instructions indicate exactly where you should make a stitch, and sometimes they do not. For example, in Row 1 of this pattern, the instructions do both:

Ch3 (counts as first dc throughout), 1dc in each st to last 5 sts, 3hdc, 2sc, turn.

Part of the instructions tell you exactly where to make your stitches (one double crochet in each stitch until you have only 5 stitches left). Where it is not specified (3hdc, 2sc), you can assume that each of the three half double crochets are worked into the following three stitches, and the two single crochets are worked into the two stitches after that. For all patterns where the exact stitches to work into are not specified, you can assume you work each stitch into the following consecutive stitches, one at a time.

FINISHING

With the right sides of the fabric facing each other (so the hat appears to be inside out), use the slip stitch seaming method to seam the hat from brim to top, then cut the yarn, leaving a long end. Using a tapestry needle, weave the yarn in and out through the edge at the top of the hat (the narrower end) and gather to close.

Weave in ends and block to measurements.

a. Brim circumference: 46 (48, 51, 53) cm/ 18 (19, 20, 21)"

b. Length (with brim folded): 19 cm/7½"

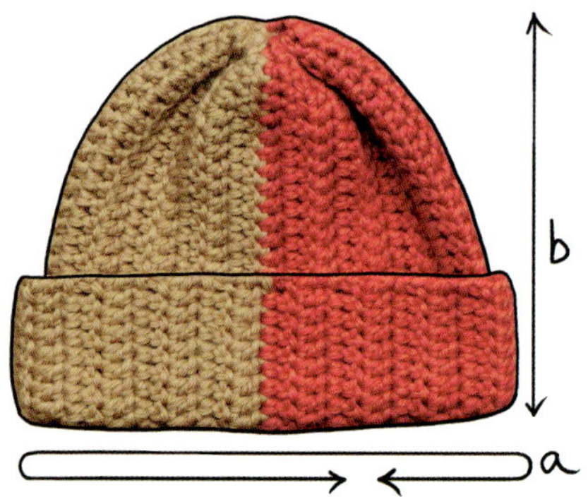

HALF DOUBLE CROCHET

Half double crochet can be worked into a chain or an already completed row of stitches. If working into a chain, you will work the first stitch into the third chain from your hook. If you have a row of stitches already completed (as pictured below), you will need a turning chain, which counts as the first stitch in the row. Work a turning chain (chain two) if working into a new row.

1. Yarn over (catch the yarn with your hook). You will have two loops on your hook.

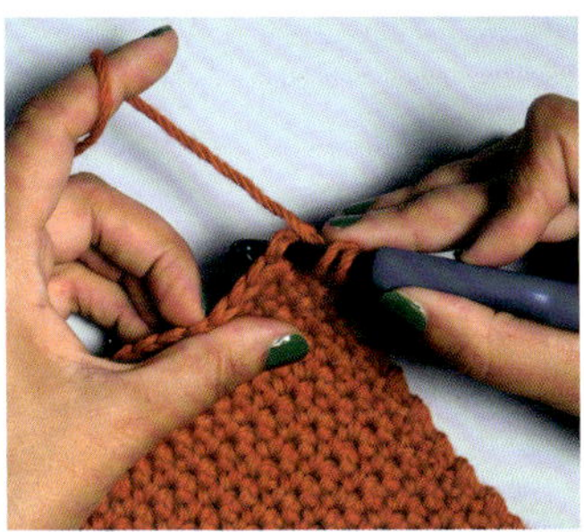

2. As your turning chain counts as a stitch, skip the first stitch and insert the hook into the following one (see page 179 if you aren't sure which stitch to work into!).

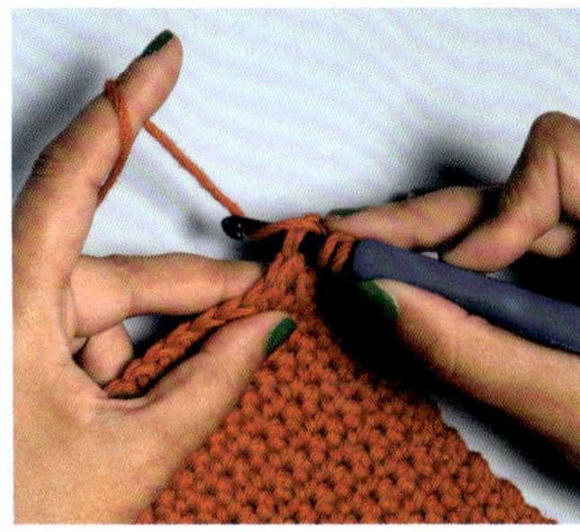

3. Yarn over (catch the yarn with your hook).

4. Pull through the fabric from back to front.

5. You will now have three loops on your hook.

6. Yarn over. You will now have four loops on your hook.

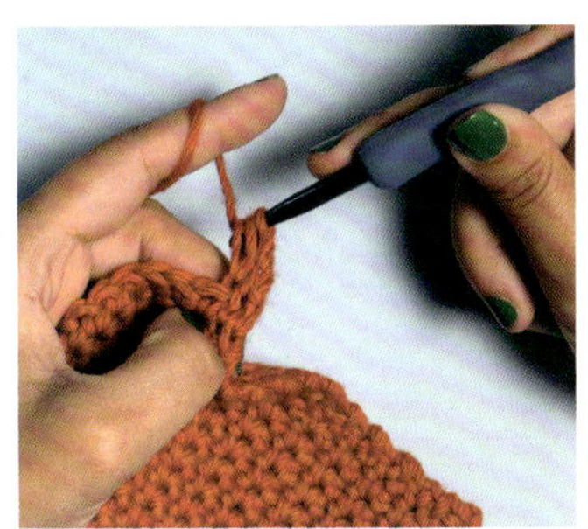

7. Pull the yarn over you just made through the last three loops on your hook.

8. Your stitch is complete.

INTRODUCTION TO GRANNY SQUARES

We couldn't write a beginner's book without a classic granny square, a crochet staple. And just like real grannies, they are clever, versatile, and have stood the test of time. These little squares use a few new skills, but we have faith in you, and we promise that you'll be addicted to them very soon—in a good way. You'll learn how to work from the center outward (instead of back and forth in rows), and how to work several stitches into one space. The stitches used in the most basic kind of granny squares are double crochet and chain stitches, two things you will already be familiar with if you've done the last two projects.

Granny squares can be made as big or small as you'd like, and once you get the hang of them, there is no limit to the way you can combine different colors and sizes of squares for your own designs. Granny squares can be used to make almost any garment or soft object you can think of, from blankets to tops to toys, or whatever your heart feels should be that much cozier.

techniques introduced:

- Magic ring (see page 64)
- Working double crochet stitches into a magic ring (see First Round of Granny Square, page 65)
- Working multiple stitches into one space (cluster stitches) (see Second Round of Granny Square, page 67)
- Joining rounds with slip stitches (see page 66)
- Weaving in ends (see page 68)

granny square

Time to try making your own granny square; we recommend practicing to get the hang of them before you move on to the following two projects.

For your practice square you will need:

- A crochet hook (we recommend US size J-10/6 mm)
- Aran yarn, 7 m/77 yards (we recommend Kremke Soul Wool the Merry Merino 70, 1 ball)

PATTERN

make magic ring

Round 1: Ch3 (counts as first dc throughout), 2dc into magic ring, [ch3, 3dc into magic ring] 3 times, ch3, sl st into top of beg 3-ch to join. *4 3-dc clusters, 4 3-ch sps*

Round 2: Ch3, 2dc into previous space (at base of 3-ch), *ch1, (3dc, ch3, 3dc) into next 3-ch sp; rep from * twice more, ch1, 3dc into next 3-ch sp, ch3, sl st in 3rd ch of beg 3-ch to join. *8 3-dc clusters, 4 1-ch sps, 4 3-ch sps*

Round 3: Ch3, 2dc into previous space, *ch1, 3dc into next 1-ch sp, ch1, (3dc, ch3, 3dc) into next 3-ch sp; rep from * twice more, ch1, 3dc into next 1-ch sp, ch1, 3dc into next 3-ch sp, ch3, sl st in 3rd ch of beg 3-ch to join. *12 3-dc clusters, 8 1-ch sps, 4 3-ch sps*

Round 4: Ch3, 2dc into previous space, *ch1, [3dc into next 1-ch sp, ch1] twice, (3dc, ch3, 3dc) into next 3-ch sp; rep from * twice more, ch1, [3dc into next 1-ch sp, ch1] twice, 3dc into next 3-ch sp, ch3, sl st in 3rd ch of beg 3-ch to join. *16 3-dc clusters, 12 1-ch sps, 4 3-ch sps*

Fasten off.

magic ring

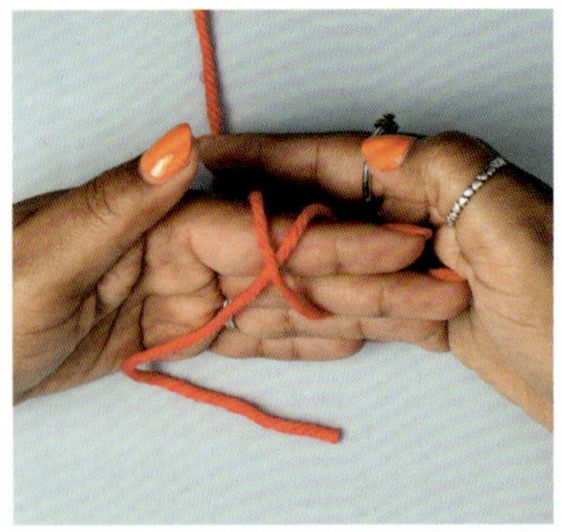

1. Begin by wrapping the yarn around your index and middle fingers as shown. The yarn should make an X, with the cut end of the yarn lying under the other end.

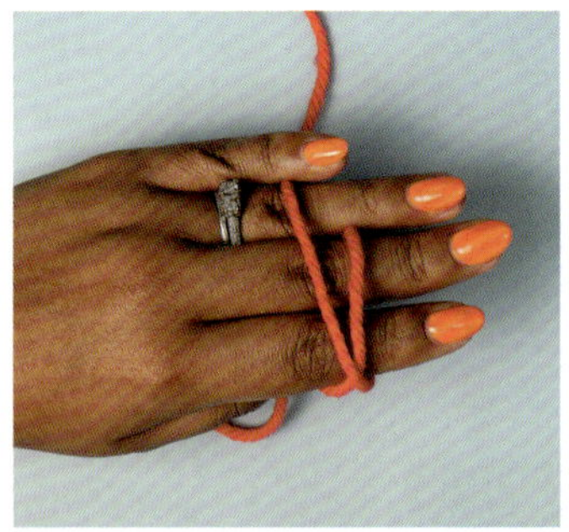

2. Flip your hand over and bring the long end of the yarn over your fingers and under your pinky to hold it in place.

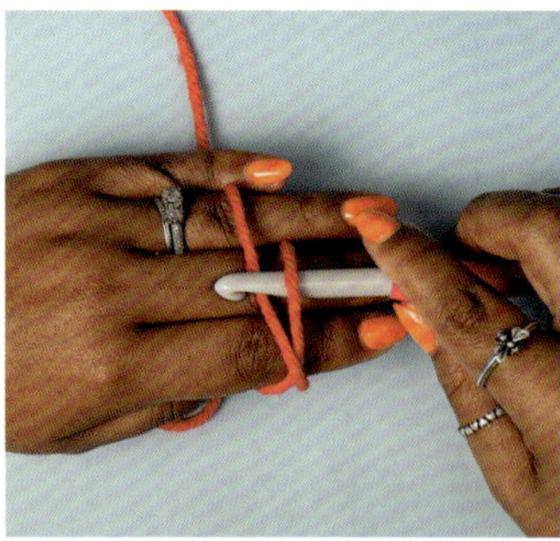

3. Insert your hook under the strand on your first two fingers and catch the other strand with the hook.

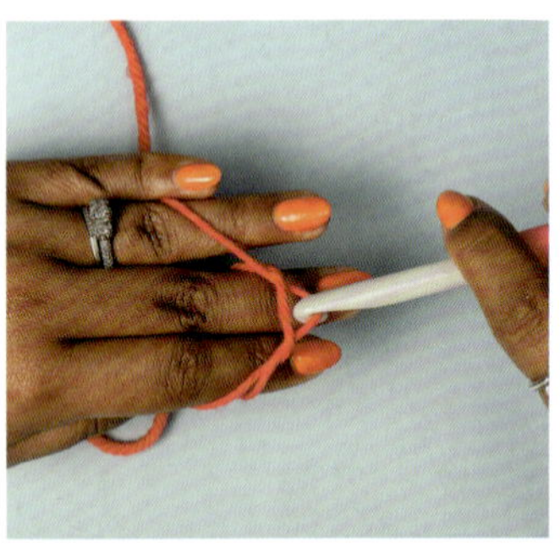

4. Pull the hook through to draw up a loop.

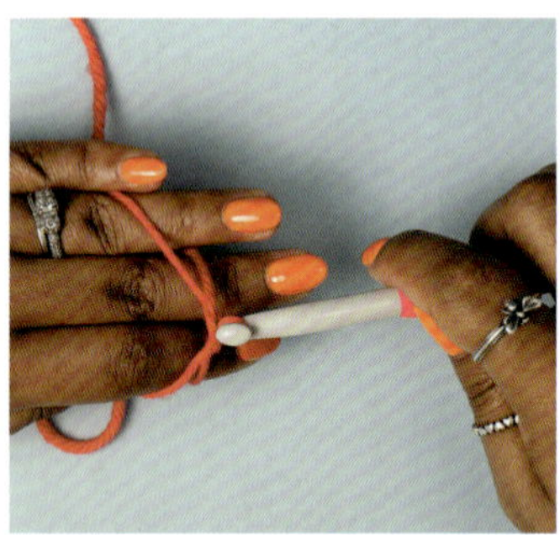

5. Twist the hook so it's in the position you would use to make a stitch.

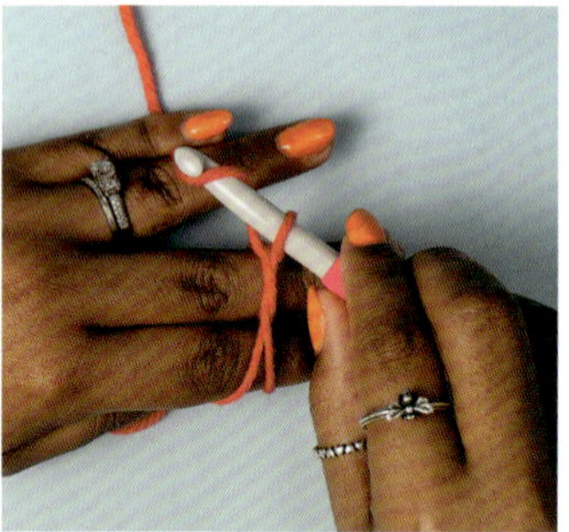

6. Still holding the loop of yarn around your fingers, catch the strand to make a yarn over. You will now have two loops on your hook.

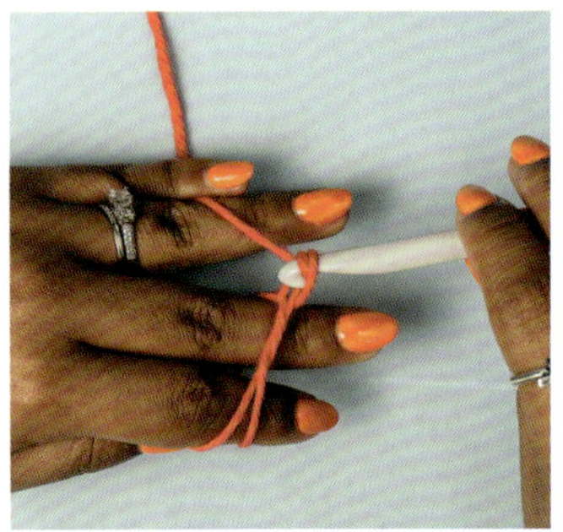

7. Draw the yarn over through the first loop on your hook.

8. The first chain in your magic ring is complete.

first round of granny square

1. You have made a magic ring and your first chain stitch. You are ready to begin round 1! Don't forget you can tighten your magic ring by pulling the yarn tail, but don't tighten it too much, as you need to be able to get your hook in.

2. Work two more chain stitches so you have a 3-ch (counts as a double crochet). Yarn over. You will now work a double crochet into the ring by inserting your hook following the path shown by the arrow.

3. With the hook inserted into the ring, work your next yarn over.

4. Pull up the loop through the ring. You should have three loops on your hook.

5. Complete this double crochet.

6. Work another double crochet in the same way, and then three chain stitches, and you have completed your first 3-dc cluster, and your first corner (created by the chain stitches)! Continue to follow your pattern until you have four clusters like this one. That's your first round completed.

joining rounds using a slip stitch

You've finished your round! All that's left is to join your last stitch to the first one to make the round continuous. You do this using a slip stitch.

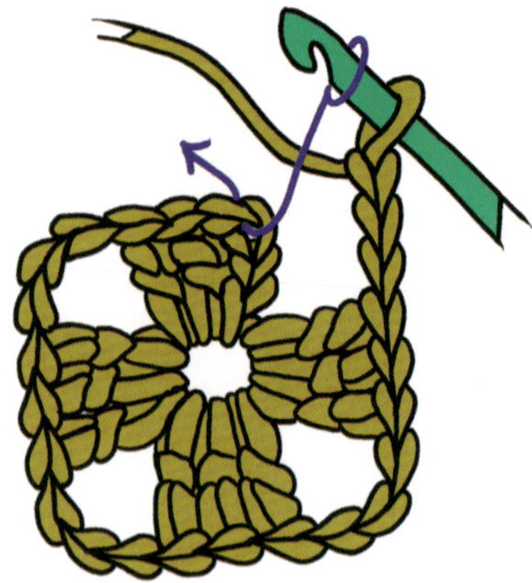

1. Insert your hook into the top of the 3-ch from the beginning of the round, following the path shown.

2. Yarn over and pull it through the top of the 3-ch.

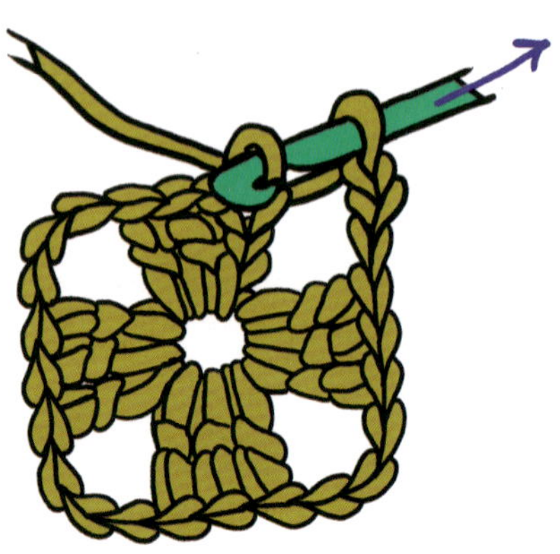

3. Now pull that same loop through the next loop on your hook.

4. Your slip stitch join is complete!

second round of granny square

You will now begin working into corner spaces. You will work into these the same way you work into chain spaces (they are just chain spaces that are at the corner!).

1. Chain 3 (this counts as the first double crochet stitch).

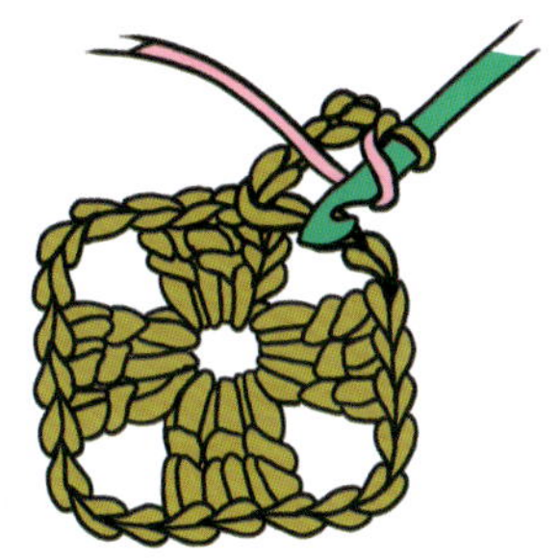

2. To work the next double crochet in your cluster, wrap yarn as shown (yarn over), and insert your hook into the previous chain space.

3. Yarn over.

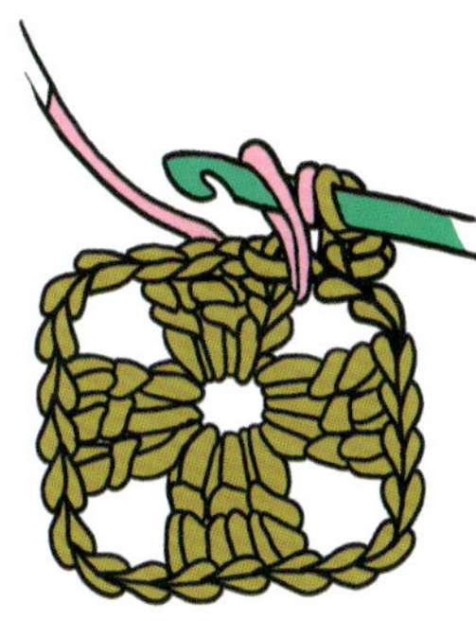

4. Pull up a loop. You will have three loops on your hook.

5. Complete your double crochet. You'll see it sits just behind the 3-ch.

6. Complete your third double crochet in the cluster, working into the same chain space.

7. Chain 1, then begin working into the next corner space by working a yarn over, then inserting your hook through the corner space and working a yarn over again as shown.

8. Complete the double crochet.

9. Continue working your double crochet cluster in the chain space and continue your granny square as instructed in the pattern.

weaving in ends: granny squares

weaving in the edge tails

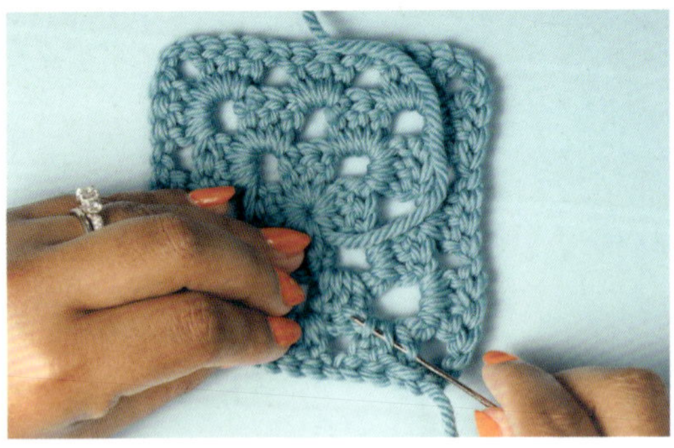

1. With the wrong side (back) of the granny square facing up, thread the tail onto a tapestry needle and skim the surface of the nearest cluster of stitches with the needle. You can insert the needle under whole strands of yarn, or through the middle of the strands of yarn, splitting the yarn. Both ways are acceptable.

2. Pull the needle and yarn through.

3. Insert the needle back in the opposite direction and pull the yarn through again.

4. Cut the yarn close to where it came out of the square. You can leave a tiny bit of excess, which will be pulled back into the square with use.

weaving in the center tails

The tail at the center of the square is worked similarly, but into the round 1 stitches, as shown at left.

project 3

MAMGU

Granny Square Soap Cozy

project 3:

GRANNY SQUARE SOAP COZY

You've made a classic granny square. Yay! (If you have not yet made a granny square, see page 62.) But what do you do with it if you don't want to make a whole blanket or garment yet? We think this is a great way to practice your squares and seaming on a much smaller project, which will brighten up a bathroom to no end. It will also solve the problem of where to put your soap, as well as doubling as a washcloth your soap can live inside of. Win-win.

note: We highly recommend using a cotton or linen yarn for this project because animal fibers like wool will become felted when wet and agitated (as this would be if used as a washcloth). Wet wool also isn't always the softest next to the skin. Unlike wool, cotton and linen wash and dry well by machine too.

notes on construction:

This cozy is created by making two granny squares and seaming them, leaving one side open to pop your soap into. You then rejoin your yarn to one corner and work chain stitches to create a loop.

techniques you need to know:

- Granny squares (see page 62)

techniques introduced:

- Seaming granny squares using mattress stitch (see page 76)
- Creating a chain stitch hanging loop (see Chain Loop Tutorial, page 75)

top tip: measuring your gauge in a granny square

Because a granny square is worked from the center out, it can be hard to figure out how to measure your gauge. Since granny squares are (usually) already little squares, and most patterns will list the size you are aiming at for each square itself, we recommend working to that rather than a row and stitch gauge. This will certainly work for the granny square patterns in this book.

pattern 3
MAMGU
soap cozy

One size: 10 cm/4" x 10 cm/4"

Yarn: Hobbii Rainbow 8/6 (sport weight; 100% cotton; 105 m/115 yds per 50-g/1.75-oz ball)

Shade: Almond (89); 1 ball

Also shown in Pastel Mint (25) and Light Purple (40)

OR approx 35 m/38 yds of DK weight yarn

Gauge: 1 granny square motif = 10 cm/4" by 10 cm/4" using US 7/4.5 mm hook, after blocking

Hook: US 7/4.5 mm

Always use a hook size that will result in the correct gauge after blocking.

Notions: Tapestry needle

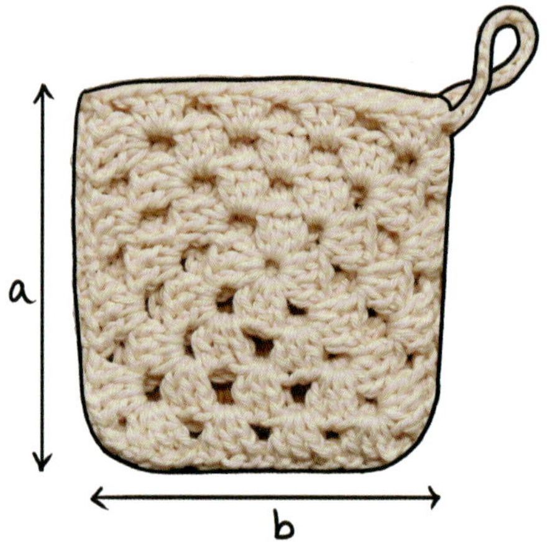

PATTERN

Granny Square (make two)

Make magic ring.

Round 1 (RS): Ch3 (counts as first dc throughout), 2dc into magic ring, [ch3, 3dc into magic ring] 3 times, ch3, sl st into top of beg 3-ch to join. *4 3-dc clusters, 4 3-ch sps*

Round 2: Ch3, 2dc into previous space (at base of 3-ch), *ch1, (3dc, ch3, 3dc) into next 3-ch sp; rep from * twice more, ch1, 3dc into next 3-ch sp, ch3, sl st in 3rd ch of beg 3-ch to join. *8 3-dc clusters, 4 1-ch sps, 4 3-ch sps*

Round 3: Ch3, 2dc into previous space, *ch1, 3dc into next 1-ch sp, ch1, (3dc, ch3, 3dc) into next 3-ch sp; rep from * twice more, ch1, 3dc into next 1-ch sp, ch1, 3dc into next 3-ch sp, ch3, sl st in 3rd ch of beg 3-ch to join. *12 3-dc clusters, 8 1-ch sps, 4 3-ch sps*

Round 4: Ch3, 2dc into previous space, *ch1, [3dc into next 1-ch sp, ch1] twice, (3dc, ch3, 3dc) into next 3-ch sp; rep from * twice more, ch1, [3dc into next 1-ch sp, ch1] twice, 3dc into next 3-ch sp, ch3, sl st in 3rd ch of beg 3-ch to join. *16 3-dc clusters, 12 1-ch sps, 4 3-ch sps*

Fasten off.

FINISHING

With WS together, seam three sides of the squares together using mattress stitch (see page 76), leaving one side open. Rejoin yarn at one of the corners of the opening, ch15 (or more if you'd like a longer hanging loop), and rejoin yarn using a sl st in the same corner to create your hanging loop.

Fasten off and weave in ends.

a. Length: 10 cm/4"
b. Width: 10 cm/4"

chain loop tutorial

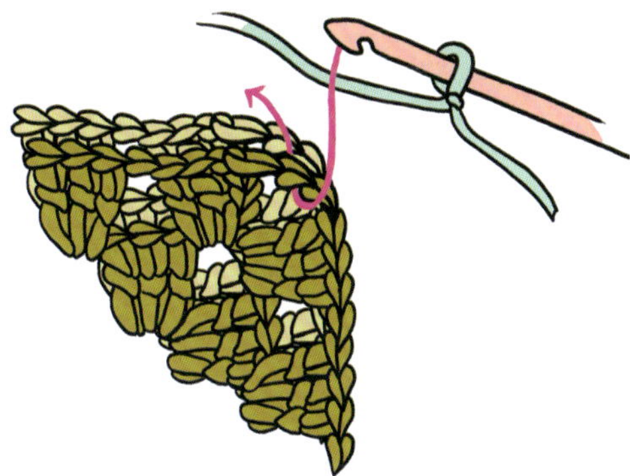

1. Start by rejoining your yarn using a slip stitch: make a slip knot and place it on your hook. With the opening of the soap cozy at the top, insert your hook into the corner space closest to you as shown. Do not insert the hook through both corner spaces!

2. To work the slip stitch, pull up a loop through the corner.

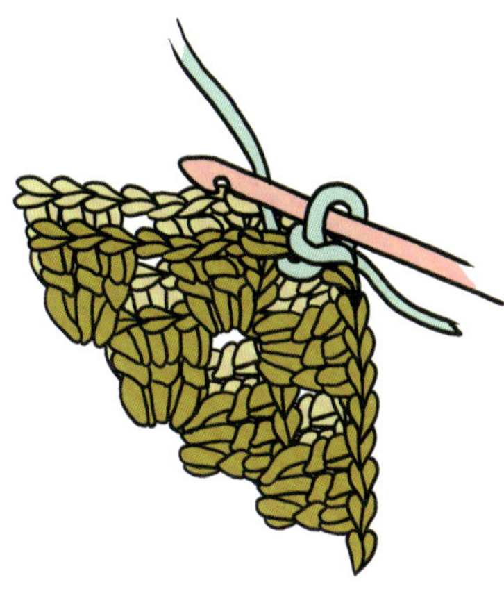

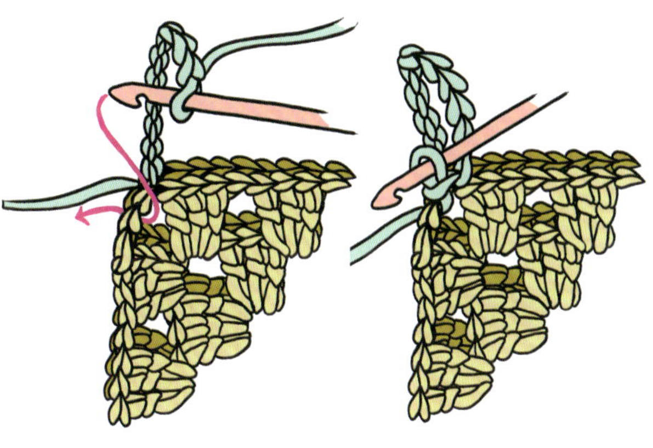

3. Complete your slip stitch by pulling the loop you just made through the slip knot.

4. Work your required number of chain stitches (we have suggested 15 in the pattern but you can work more or less if you'd like a bigger or smaller loop). Then turn the soap cozy so the granny square on the other side is facing you. Insert your hook through the corresponding corner behind the one where you started. Complete your slip stitch to join the loop.

Cut yarn, fasten off, and weave in ends.

seaming granny squares using mattress stitch

1. To seam granny squares together using mattress stitch, lay two squares side by side, with the wrong sides (backs) facing up. Using a long length of yarn (about two times the length of the seam), insert a threaded tapestry needle under just the uppermost strand of one stitch at the corner of one square and draw the yarn through gently.

2. Insert the tapestry needle into the corresponding stitch on the other square in the same way. Gently draw the yarn through.

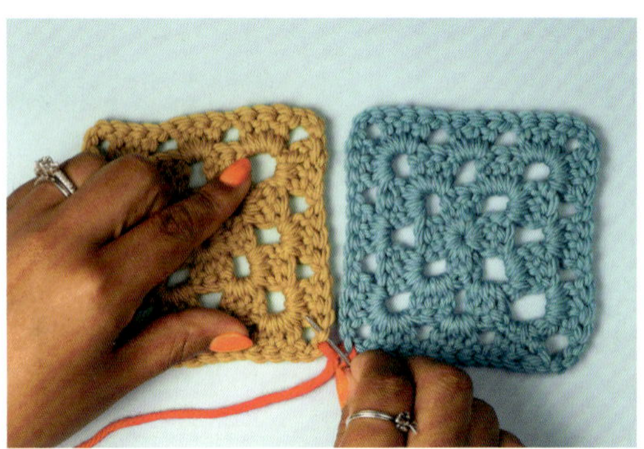

3. Insert the tapestry needle back into the first side in the same way, into the next stitch up, under the uppermost strand of that stitch.

4. Continue working back and forth between the squares as established.

5. The seaming yarn will zigzag back and forth between the squares as pictured.

6. Every so often, pull on both ends of the yarn to draw the seam closed.

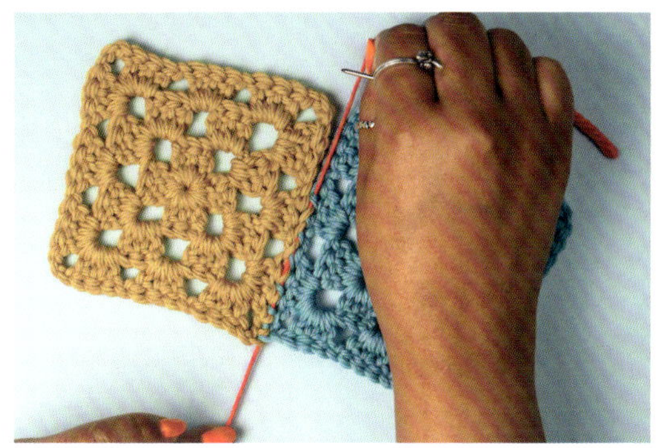

7. The yarn will be almost completely hidden. Continue seaming and pulling the seam closed as needed.

8. This is what the seam looks like from the front—nearly invisible. If seaming many blocks (as for a blanket), you can seam squares together to form strips and then seam those strips together in the same way.

project 4

SOPHIA

Granny Square Blanket

project 4:
GRANNY SQUARE BLANKET

This little lap or baby blanket is a nice, approachable size for a first blanket project. You make all your squares (perfect little mini, bite-size crochet snacks for evenings) and then seam them together. We love the layout for this blanket; it's a play on a check fabric, making the most of the little squares it's made up from. You can play with your own color possibilities using the template on page 83, or even do stripes or a simple check. Or all one color. There are no bad choices.

notes on construction:
This blanket is created by making 81 granny squares and seaming them together.

techniques you need to know:
- Granny squares (see page 62)
- Mattress stitch seaming for granny squares (see page 76)

techniques introduced:
- Following a layout plan (see pages 82–83)
- Seaming a large project (see page 76)

note: You are very welcome to use the exact same colors and layout of squares as we have for the version pictured here. But you might feel adventurous and want to create your own palette. We have included a template on page 83 so you can get out your colored pencils or markers to design your own color story. What you decide to do will dictate how many squares of each color to make. Of course, you might just decide to wing it and choose colors as you go. We fully support this approach too.

top tip: seaming

We used mattress stitch (see page 76) to seam the squares in this blanket, but you might choose to use a slip stitch seam (see page 23). There are many ways to seam granny squares, and you'll come to know your own preferences with time and experience. Mattress stitch is nearly imperceptible from the right side of the blanket, but for reference, we used the purple shade for seaming—simply because it was the color we had the most of left over after making the squares.

When cutting a length of yarn for mattress stitch, keep in mind that you don't necessarily want a strand long enough to seam the entire length of the blanket. The yarn would be quite long and have the tendency to get tangled. We recommend cutting a strand about twice the length of your forearm. Cut a new length as needed.

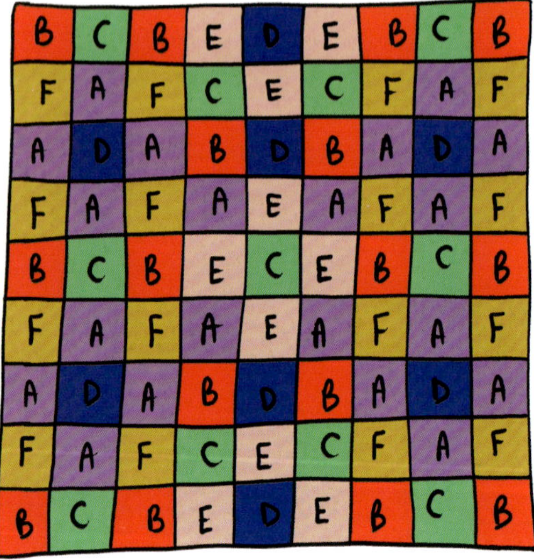

pattern 4

SOPHIA granny square blanket

One size: 72 cm/28¼" square

Yarn: Manos del Uruguay Ideal (worsted weight; 100% Polwarth wool; 200 m/219 yds per 100-g/3.5-oz skein)

Shades:

Yarn A: Nymph; 2 skeins

Yarn B: Zinnia; 1 skein

Yarn C: Tahiti; 1 skein

Yarn D: Royal; 1 skein

Yarn E: Peach Blossom; 1 skein

Yarn F: Icarus; 1 skein

OR approx:

Yarn A: 237 m/259 yds of worsted weight yarn

Yarn B: 174 m/190 yds of worsted weight yarn

Yarn C: 120 m/131 yds of worsted weight yarn

Yarn D: 87 m/95 yds of worsted weight yarn

Yarn E: 109 m/119 yds of worsted weight yarn

Yarn F: 174 m/190 yds of worsted weight yarn

Gauge: 1 granny square = 8 cm/3¼" using US H-8/5 mm hook, after blocking

Hook: US H-8/5 mm

Always use a hook size that will result in the correct gauge after blocking.

Notions: Tapestry needle

PATTERN

Make magic ring.

Round 1 (RS): Ch3 (counts as first dc throughout), 2dc into magic ring, [ch3, 3dc into magic ring] 3 times, ch3, sl st in 3rd ch of beg 3-ch to join. *4 3-dc clusters, 4 3-ch sps*

Round 2: Ch3, 2dc into previous space (at base of 3-ch), *ch1, (3dc, ch3, 3dc) into next 3-ch sp; rep from * twice more, ch1, 3dc into next 3-ch sp, ch3, sl st in 3rd ch of beg 3-ch to join. *8 3-dc clusters, 4 1-ch sps, 4 3-ch sps*

Round 3: Ch3, 2dc into previous space, *ch1, 3dc into next 1-ch sp, ch1, (3dc, ch3, 3dc) into next 3-ch sp; rep from * twice more, ch1, 3dc into next 1-ch sp, ch1, 3dc into next 3-ch sp, ch3, sl st in 3rd ch of beg 3-ch to join. *12 3-dc clusters, 8 1-ch sps, 4 3-ch sps*

Fasten off.

make granny squares as follows:

Yarn A (purple) x 20
Yarn B (red) x 16
Yarn C (green) x 11
Yarn D (blue) x 8
Yarn E (pink) x 10
Yarn F (yellow) x 16
(81 squares total for 9 x 9–square blanket)

FINISHING

Weave in all the ends of your squares. Using Yarn A, seam them in the layout as shown in the diagram on the opposite page—we used mattress stitch for this sample.

a. Length: 72 cm/28"
b. Width: 72 cm/28"

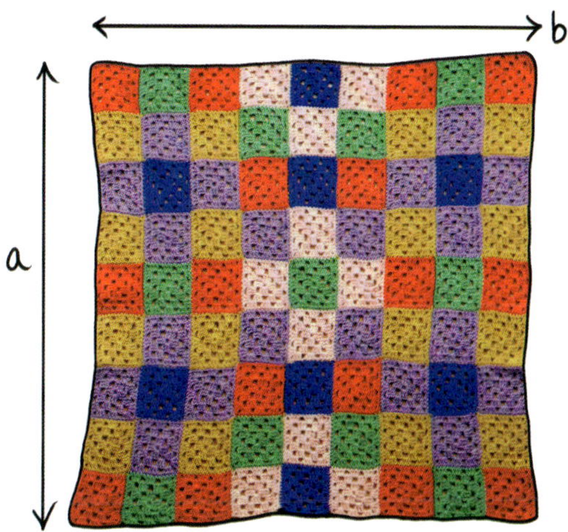

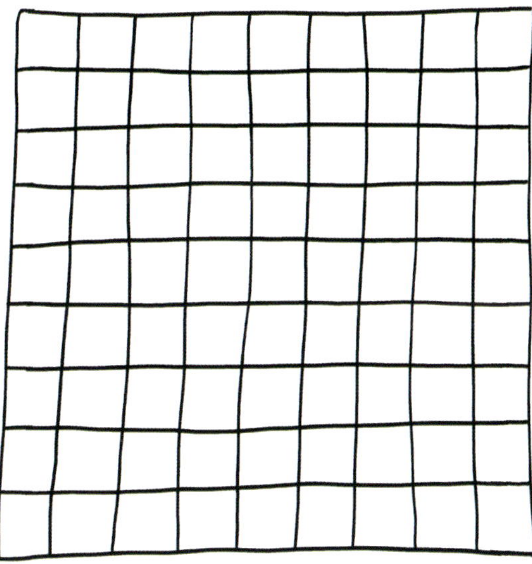

Use this template to plan your own color palette.

project 5

SARA

Kerchief/Bandana

project 5:
KERCHIEF/BANDANA

This versatile little thing is equally happy as a kerchief, a headscarf, or even a bow. This pattern will teach some simple increases and decreases to create the points. If you want something longer, it's easy to lengthen, but just remember you might need more yarn.

notes on construction:
This kerchief is worked from tip to tip, starting with just three stitches and increasing, then decreasing back to three again to finish.

techniques you need to know:
- Chain (see page 12)
- Double crochet (see page 46)

techniques introduced:
- Double crochet increases (see page 90)
- Double crochet decreases (dc2tog, see page 91)
- Working a short chain

top tip: measuring length

As we mentioned, you can make this little scarf as long as you want. Be aware, however, that crochet fabric can often grow—meaning, when washed, the yarn might expand, or the stitches themselves might loosen up. This is why it's great to make a gauge swatch and then wash and block that swatch to see how the yarn and stitches behave (see page 31). Measure your gauge swatch before and after blocking to understand how much your project might change after washing. While the difference might be negligible for a small project like this, it will become crucial for something like a sweater. Now would be a great time to practice.

pattern 5

SARA kerchief/bandana

Sizes: 1(2)

Finished dimensions: 8.5 cm/3¼" wide x 76 (86) cm/ 30 (34)" long

Yarn: Pom Pom x Hobbii Garland (worsted weight; 70% cotton, 30% alpaca; 105 m/114 yds per 50-g/ 1.75-oz ball)

Shade: Muse; 1 ball

Also shown in Heart of Glass and Foal (longer sample)

OR approx 80 (92) m/88 (101) yds of worsted weight yarn

Gauge: 18 sts & 8.5 rows = 10 cm/4" in double crochet using US 7/4.5 mm hook, after blocking

Hook: US 7/4.5 mm

Always use a hook size that will result in the correct gauge after blocking.

Notions: Tapestry needle, locking stitch marker

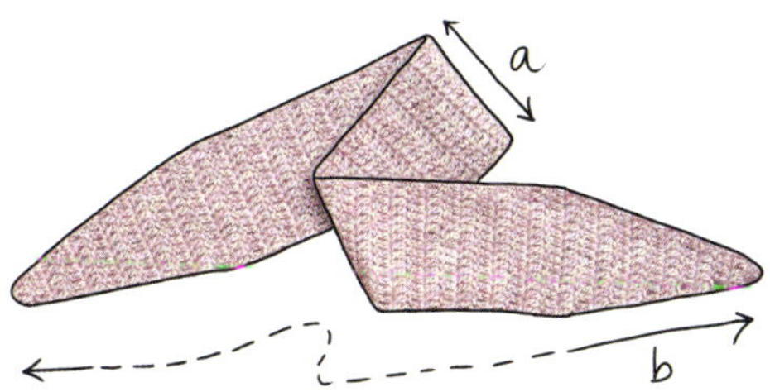

PATTERN

Ch4.

Set-up row: 2dc in 4th ch from hook (missed 3-ch counts as dc), turn. *3 sts*

Row 1 (RS): Ch3 (counts as first dc throughout), 1dc in same st (at base of 3-ch), 1dc, 2dc in last st, turn. *5 sts*

Row 2 (WS): Ch3, 1dc in each st to end, turn.

note: Place a locking stitch marker to identify the RS of the fabric.

Row 3: Ch3, 1dc in same st, 1dc in each st to last st, 2dc in last st, turn. *2 sts inc*

Repeat Rows 2 and 3 a further 4 times. *15 sts*

Next row: Ch3, 1dc in each st to end, turn.

Repeat last row until kerchief measures approx 61 (71) cm/24 (28)" or 15 cm/6" less than desired length (just remember that if you make it longer, you may need more yarn).

Start to work decreases as follows:

Row 1 (RS): Ch2 (does not count as dc throughout), sk st at base of 2-ch, 1dc in each st to last 2 sts, dc2tog, turn. *2 sts dec*

Row 2 (WS): Ch3, 1dc in each st to end (do not work into beg 2-ch of previous row), turn.

Repeat Rows 1 and 2 until 3 sts rem.

Next row: Ch2, dc2tog.

Fasten off.

FINISHING

Weave in ends and block to measurements.

a. Width: 8.5 cm/3¼"
b. Length: 76 (86) cm/30 (34)"

increase—
working two double crochets into one stitch

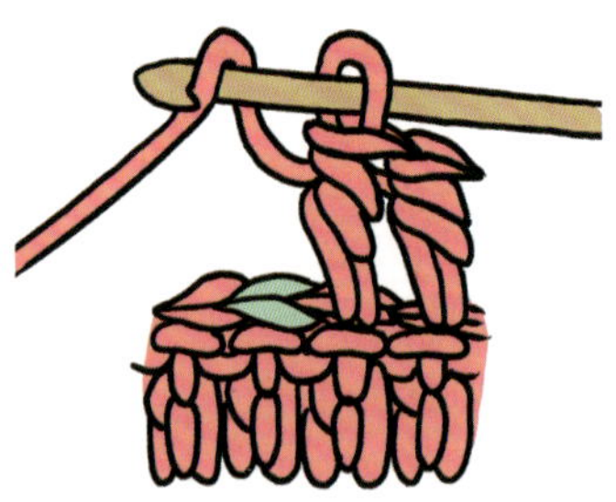

1. To increase the number of stitches you have in a row or round, you can work two stitches into one. The stitch highlighted in green is where the increase will happen: two stitches will be worked into it.

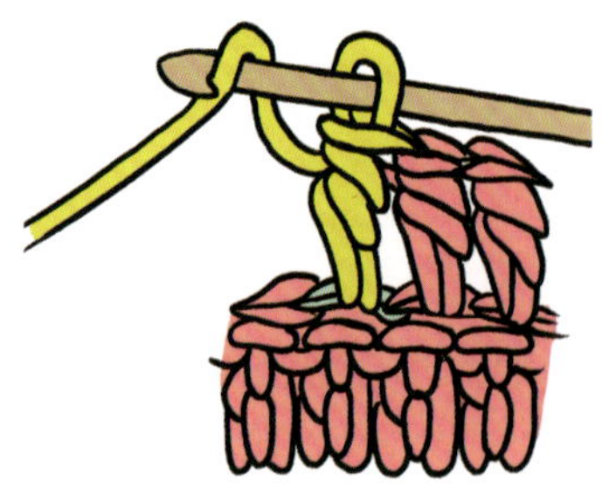

2. Work one double crochet stitch and yarn over to begin the next double crochet.

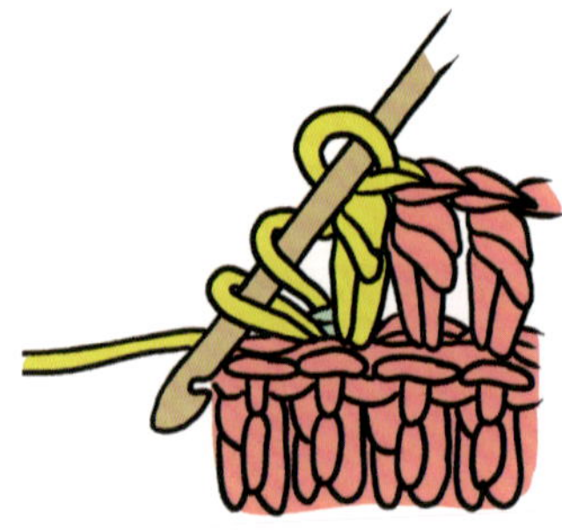

3. Insert your hook in the same stitch and pull up a loop.

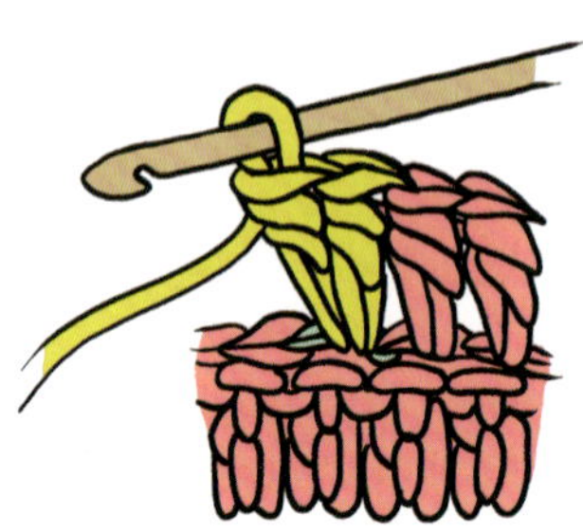

4. Finish your second double crochet. You have increased one stitch!

increase—
working into first stitch after turning chain

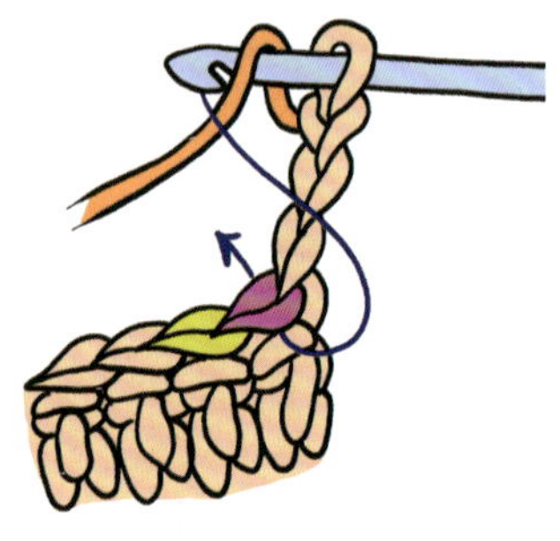

1. Usually when working in double crochet, you skip the first stitch after a turning chain, because the turning chain counts as that first stitch. But to work an increase at the beginning of a row you *will* work into that first stitch.

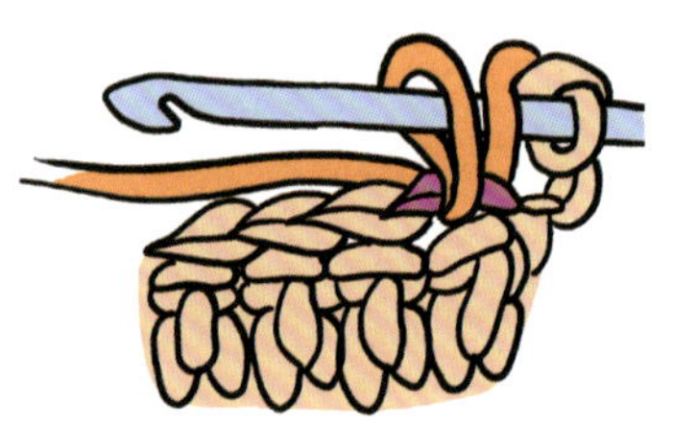

2. Yarn over and insert your hook into the first stitch (at the base of the turning chain).

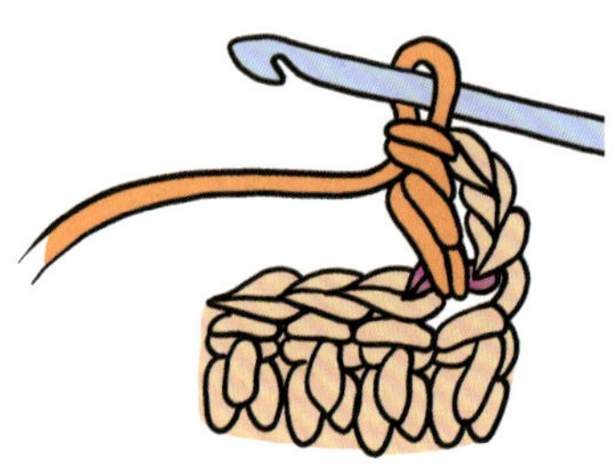

3. Complete your double crochet stitch. As you can see, your stitch sits right at the base of the turning chain. You have increased one stitch!

decrease—
double crochet two together

1. To double crochet two together (dc2tog) work into the next two stitches (highlighted in green).

2. Yarn over and insert the hook into the first stitch. Pull a loop through. You will have two loops on your hook.

3. Yarn over again and pull the loop through the next two loops on your hook. You have completed the first half of a double crochet stitch.

4. Now repeat steps two and three in the next stitch along. You now have two partially made double crochet stitches.

5. Yarn over, and pull the loop through the next three loops on your hook.

6. You have completed your dc2tog. In place of two stitches you now have one!

project 6

ASHLEY

Market Bag and Bottle Holder

project 6:
MARKET BAG AND BOTTLE HOLDER

A market bag is such a useful little thing! Perfect to squish into your handbag or backpack on your way out the door, but capacious enough to carry a lot. This pattern will build confidence with increases while also teaching you a few new tricks (and one new stitch).

The bottle holder is a smaller version of the same pattern, with a few tweaks to the top and the strap. It's useful if you are out and about and don't want to take a whole bag just for your water. We all know it's essential to stay hydrated, so this little holder will come in handy time and again. We've also been considering all the other possibilities for this holder—wine, a carton of milk, a thermos, a baguette. Whatever your heart desires and your imagination can muster.

notes on construction:
Both of these patterns start with a magic ring and work increases evenly in rounds to create the base. Then you work a simple mesh, with an exciting new stitch—the treble crochet. The top of the bag is worked with decreases, and then the straps are created by working chains, which are then joined back to the top of the bag with slip stitches to strengthen them.

The bottle holder is worked similarly until you get to the top. It has just one strap, which is crocheted separately and then joined by sewing it to the holder, and it's also made thicker using double crochet rather than slip stitches.

techniques you need to know:
- Chain (see page 12)
- Magic ring (see page 64)
- Double crochet (see page 46)
- Increasing (see page 90)
- Joining rounds with slip stitch (see page 66)

techniques introduced:
- Treble crochet (see page 100)
- Slip stitch into a chain (see page 103)
- Slip stitch into a chain space to move beginning of round (see page 102)

note: Use a strong, sturdy fiber like cotton or linen for this project. The last thing you want is heavy canned items or jars breaking through your bag.

pattern 6.1

ASHLEY market bag

One size: 40 cm/15¾" deep (not including handles) x 38 cm/15" wide (at widest point)

Yarn: Purl Soho Cotton Chirp 4-color set (DK weight; 100% cotton; 53 m/58 yds per 25-g/.88-oz mini ball OR 212 m/232 yds per Heirloom White 100-g/3.5-oz ball)

SINGLE COLOR VERSION

Shade: Heirloom White; 2 balls

MULTICOLOR VERSION

note: Shades used are from the Inchworm 4-color set and Mint Citrus 4-color set.

Shades:

Yarn A: Lawn Green; 1 ball

Yarn B: Dill Pickle; 1 ball

Yarn C: Green Pomelo; 1 ball

Yarn D: Chartreuse Yellow; 1 ball

Yarn E: Yellow Parakeet; 1 ball

OR approx 318 m/347 yds total of DK weight yarn

Gauge: Rounds 1–8 = 10 cm/4" in double crochet using US H-8/5 mm hook, after blocking

Hook: US H-8/5 mm

Always use a hook size that will result in the correct gauge after blocking.

Notions: Tapestry needle, locking stitch markers

top tip!

Remember that your bag will stretch a lot when it's filled. If you want to check if it's the size you want, we recommend popping a stitch marker into the live stitch to secure it, filling the bag, and seeing if it suits your needs. Add more rounds from the Mesh section of the pattern if needed.

PATTERN

note: If you are working the **Multicolor Version**, start with yarn A.

Make magic ring.

Set-up round (RS): Ch3 (counts as dc throughout), 11dc into magic ring, sl st in 3rd ch of beg 3-ch to join, pull tail firmly to close ring. *12 sts*

You will now start to work increases to increase the circumference of the base of the bag:

Round 1: Ch3, 1dc into same st (at base of 3-ch), 2dc into each st to end, sl st in 3rd ch of beg 3-ch. *24 sts*

Round 2: Ch3, 1dc into same st, [1dc, 2dc into next st] 11 times, 1dc, sl st in 3rd ch of beg 3-ch. *36 sts*

Round 3: Ch3, 1dc into same st, [2dc, 2dc into next st] 11 times, 2dc, sl st in 3rd ch of beg 3-ch. *48 sts*

Round 4: Ch3, 1dc into same st, [3dc, 2dc into next st] 11 times, 3dc, sl st in 3rd ch of beg 3-ch. *60 sts*

Round 5: Ch3, 1dc into same st, [4dc, 2dc into next st] 11 times, 4dc, sl st in 3rd ch of beg 3-ch. *72 sts*

Round 6: Ch3, 1dc into same st, [5dc, 2dc into next st] 11 times, 5dc, sl st in 3rd ch of beg 3-ch. *84 sts*

Round 7: Ch3, 1dc into same st, [6dc, 2dc into next st] 11 times, 6dc, sl st in 3rd ch of beg 3-ch. *96 sts*

Round 8: Ch3, 1dc into same st, [7dc, 2dc into next st] 11 times, 7dc, sl st in 3rd ch of beg 3-ch. *108 sts*

note: If you are working the **Multicolor Version,** change to Yarn B for next round.

Round 9: Ch3, 1dc into same st, [8dc, 2dc into next st] 11 times, 8dc, sl st in 3rd ch of beg 3-ch. *120 sts*

Round 10: Ch3, 1dc into same st, [9dc, 2dc into next st] 11 times, 9dc, sl st in 3rd ch of beg 3-ch. *132 sts*

Round 11: Ch3, 1dc into same st, [10dc, 2dc into next st] 11 times, 10dc, sl st in 3rd ch of beg 3-ch. *144 sts*

Round 12: Ch3, 1dc in each st to end, sl st in 3rd ch of beg 3-ch.

note: If you are working the **Multicolor Version,** change to yarn C for next round.

Round 13: Ch3, 1dc in each st to end, sl st in 3rd ch of beg 3-ch.

mesh

note: If you are working the **Multicolor Version,** change to yarn D after 3 rounds of Mesh, and then to yarn E after 7 total rounds of Mesh.

Round 1: Ch4 (counts as tr), [ch1, sk 1 st, 1tr in next st] to last st, ch1, sk 1 st, sl st in 4th ch of beg 4-ch.

Repeat Round 1 a further 8 times or until bag is approx 1.5 cm/½" less than desired height without Handles (remember that if you make the bag bigger, you might need more yarn).

top and handles

Round 1: Sl st into first ch sp, ch3 (counts as dc), 1dc into each ch sp to end, sl st in 3rd ch of beg 3-ch to join. *72 sts*

Round 2: Ch1 (counts as sc throughout), 1sc in each st to end, sl st in beg 1-ch to join.

Round 3: Ch1, 5sc, ch82, sk next 24 sc, 12sc, ch82, sk next 24 sc, 6sc, sl st in beg 1-ch to join.

Round 4: Ch1, 5sc, sl st in each of next 82 ch for first Handle, 12sc, sl st in each of next 82 ch for second Handle, 6sc, sl st in beg 1-ch to join.

Fasten off.

FINISHING

Weave in ends and block to measurements.

a. Depth (including handles): 63 cm/24¾"
b. Depth (not including handles): 40 cm/15¾"
c. Width (at widest point): 38 cm/15"

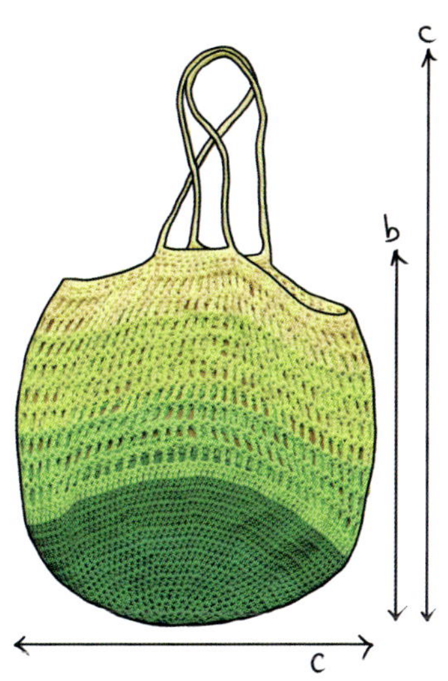

pattern 6.2

ASHLEY bottle holder

One size: 10 cm/4" wide x 16 cm/6¼" deep (not including strap)

Yarn: Purl Soho Cotton Chirp 4-color set (DK weight; 100% cotton; 53 m/58 yds per 25-g/.88-oz mini ball)

note: Shades used are from the Apple Blossom 4-color set.

Shades:

Yarn A: Hibiscus Pink; 1 ball

Yarn B: Peach Bisque; 1 ball

OR approx:

Yarn A: 28 m/31 yds of DK weight yarn

Yarn B: 46 m/50 yds of DK weight yarn

Gauge: Rounds 1–7 = 10 cm/4" using US 7/4.5 mm hook, after blocking

Hook: US 7/4.5 mm

Always use a hook size that will result in the correct gauge after blocking.

Notions: Tapestry needle, locking stitch markers

note: The bottle holder is worked from the center of the bottom of the holder, increasing to create a flat circle of fabric. Then mesh is worked without increases to create the body of the bottle holder, and then a strap is added at the end. This holder holds a 6.5 cm/2½" diameter x 21 cm/8¼" tall bottle comfortably. If you have a larger bottle, you can work further increase rounds (see Market Bag pattern).

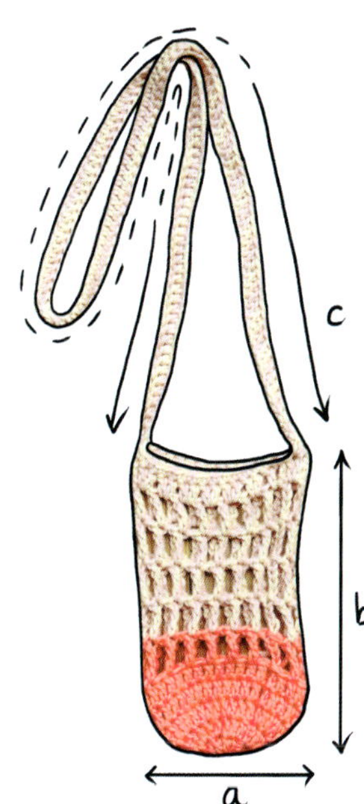

PATTERN

Using Yarn A make magic ring.

Set-up round (RS): Ch3 (counts as dc throughout), 11dc into magic ring, sl st in 3rd ch of beg 3-ch to join, pull tail firmly to close ring. *12 sts*

You will now start to work increases to increase the circumference of the base:

Round 1: Ch3, 1dc into same st (at base of 3-ch), 2dc into each st to end, sl st in 3rd ch of beg 3-ch. *24 sts*

Round 2: Ch3, 1dc into same st, [1dc, 2dc into next st] 11 times, 1dc, sl st in 3rd ch of beg 3-ch. *36 sts*

note: Work further increase rounds before continuing if required (see Pattern Note).

Rounds 3 and 4: Ch3, 1dc in each st to end, sl st in 3rd ch of beg 3-ch.

mesh

Round 1: Ch4 (counts as tr), [ch1, sk 1 st, 1tr in next st] to last st, ch1, sk 1 st, sl st in 4th ch of beg 4-ch. Change to Yarn B. Repeat Round 1 a further 4 times, or until body of holder is approx 1.5 cm/½" less than desired depth.

top

Round 1: Sl st into first ch sp, ch3 (counts as dc), 1dc into same sp, 2dc into each ch sp to end, sl st in 3rd ch of beg 3-ch to join. *36 sts*

Round 2: Ch1 (counts as first sc), 1sc into each st to end, sl st in beg 1-ch to join.
Fasten off.

handle

Ch142.

Next row: 1dc in 4th ch from hook (missed 3-ch counts as dc), 1dc in each st to end. *140 sts*

Fasten off.

FINISHING

Sew ends of Handle securely to opposite sides of holder. Weave in ends and block to measurements.

a. Width: 10 cm/4"
b. Depth (not including strap): 16 cm/6¼"
c. Strap length: 43 cm/17"

TREBLE CROCHET

Treble crochet can be worked into a chain or an already completed row of stitches. If working into a chain, you will work into the fifth chain from your hook. If you have a row of stitches already completed (as pictured below), you will need a turning chain made up of four chain stitches, which counts as the first stitch in the row.

1. To work the treble crochet stitch, yarn over (catch the yarn with your hook) *twice*. You will have three loops on your hook.

2. Insert the hook into the following stitch.

3. Yarn over and pull through the fabric from back to front.

4. You will now have four loops on your hook.

5. Yarn over again. (Five loops on the hook.)

6. Pull the yarn over you just made through the next two loops on your hook. (You now have three loops on your hook.)

7. Yarn over again. (Four loops on the hook.)

8. Pull the yarn over you just made through the next two loops on your hook. (You now have two loops on your hook.)

9. Yarn over again. (Three loops on the hook.)

10. Pull the yarn over you just made through the last two loops on your hook. Your stitch is complete.

slip stitch into chain space to move beginning of round

In this instance the slip stitch is being used to move the beginning of the round.

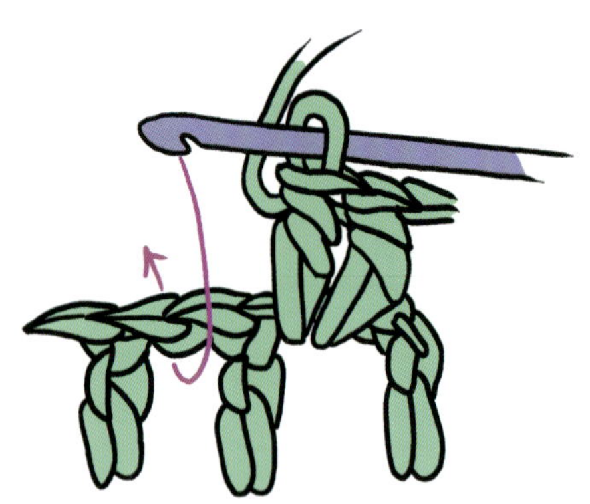

1. You will be working into the next chain space (indicated by the arrow) as shown.

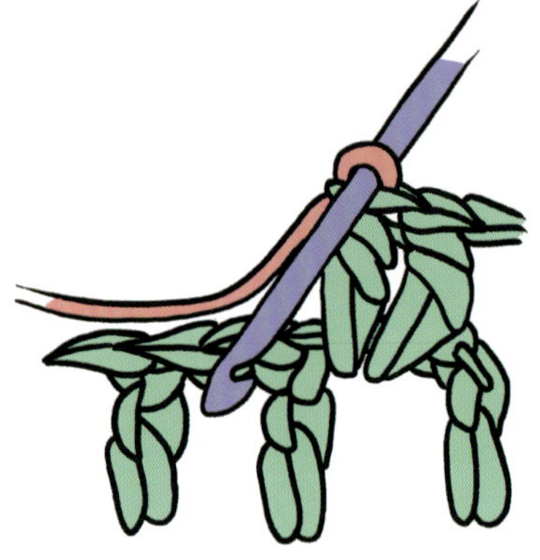

2. Insert your hook into the chain space.

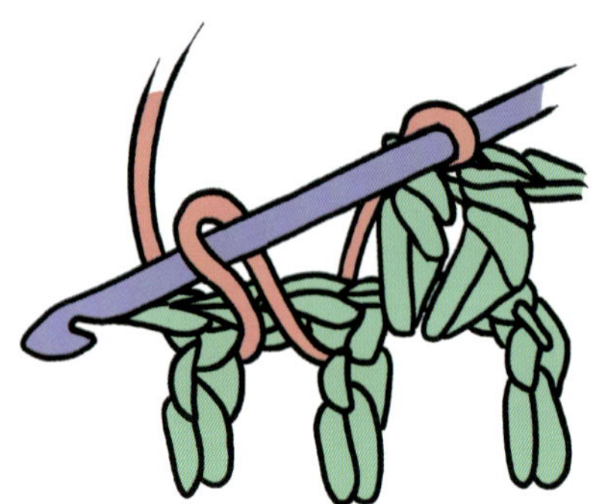

3. Pull a loop through the chain space.

4. Pull this same loop through the first loop on your hook. Your slip stitch is complete.

slip stitch into a chain

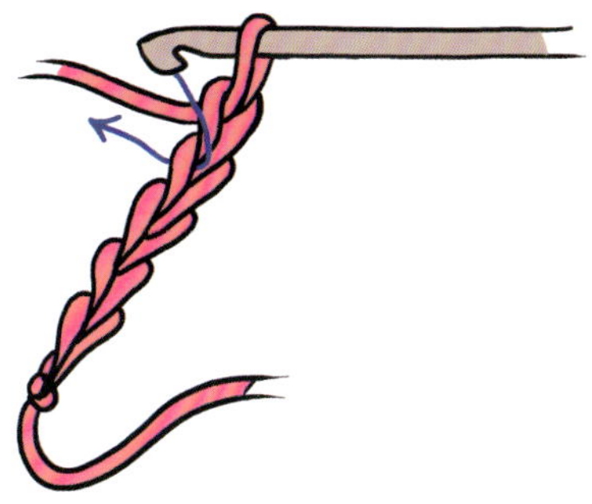

1. Insert your hook into the second chain from your hook as shown.

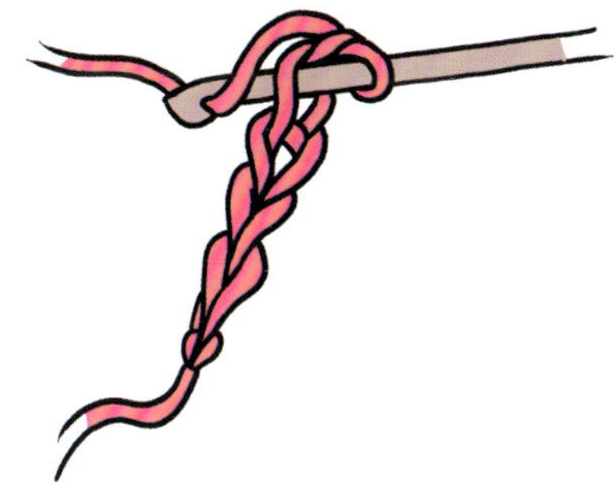

2. Yarn over your hook and pull through the chain.

3. Continue by pulling that same loop through the first loop on the hook.

4. You have completed your slip stitch.

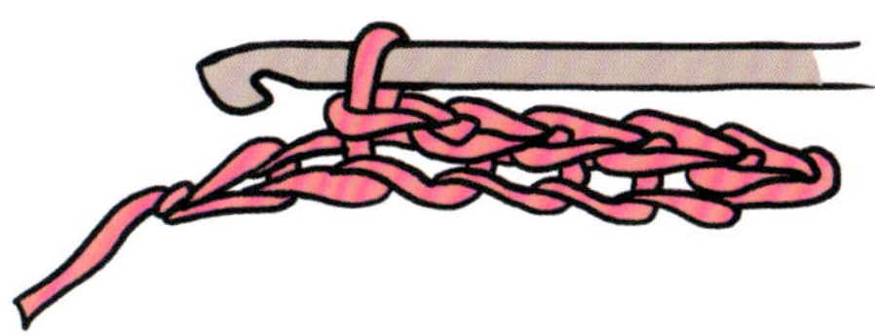

5. Continue working slip stitches into each chain as instructed.

project 7

SALSABIL

Lace Top

project 7:
LACE TOP

Using a few basic stitches, this top can either be a summery tank top, or a cozier vest to wear over longer sleeves. The only difference is the yarn you choose. The front and back are identical, with the same decreasing and increasing for the neckline. This is a fun first top with a simple stitch pattern, and as with a granny square, it features double crochet clusters and chain spaces, just applied in a different way. It's worked sideways, so you start with the underarm and work across, chaining extra stitches to create straps and working shorter rows when needed.

notes on construction:
This top is worked from side to side in rows; the front and back are the same. Pieces are seamed together at the sides and the tops of the straps to finish.

techniques you need to know:

- Chain (see page 12)
- Double crochet (see page 46)
- Increasing (see page 90)
- Decreasing (see page 91)
- Seaming (see pages 22–24)

techniques introduced:

- Measuring for fit and choosing a size (see Top Tip at left)

top tip: choosing a size

Since this is very likely your first garment, you probably need help choosing which size to make. Crochet patterns rarely match typical store-bought sizing conventions (or at least, good ones don't) because the idea is to get a custom fit for you. In garments (as opposed to accessories), typically the main body measurement to focus on is the chest (or bust) measurement. Have a friend measure the widest point at chest level for you. Measuring your own chest will give you an inaccurate reading because your arms will be in use. Then have a look at the *finished* measurement in the pattern AND the amount of ease suggested (see page 56) to determine the size you want to make.

For example, this pattern calls for 1–3" of positive ease. If your own chest circumference is 38", the final measurement of your top should be between 39–41". In this case, you'd choose the third size listed, which has a finished measurement of 41". If you decided you wanted your top to be even looser or oversized, you could go for the next size up. If you're unsure, pull out a similar top from your wardrobe that you like the fit of, measure it at the chest, and choose a size that corresponds.

top tip: using row counters

Garments tend to have a lot more rows and pattern instructions than accessories, and often you'll be instructed to repeat a set of rows multiple times. To help keep track of how many rows you've completed (especially if you need to put down your project between rows), a row counter can be really helpful. These little gadgets are a bit like those counters you see security guards use to count the number of people at large events. Click the counter every time you complete a row, and you'll always know how many you've done without having to analyze your fabric.

pattern 7

SALSABIL
lace top

stitch glossary: cluster pattern

Ch a multiple of 3+1.

For your gauge swatch you might want to ch25.

Set-up row (RS): 1dc in 4th ch from hook (missed 3-ch counts as dc), 1dc in each ch to end, turn.

Row 1 (WS): Ch3 (counts as first dc throughout), sk 1 st, 3dc in next st, [sk 2 sts, 3dc in next st] to last 2 sts, sk 1 st, 1dc in top of 3-ch, turn.

Row 2 (RS): Ch3, 1dc in each st to end, turn. Rep Rows 1 and 2 for pattern.

Sizes: 1 (2, 3, 4, 5, 6, 7, 8, 9)

Finished chest (fullest point) circumference: 78.5 (89, 104, 114.5, 124.5, 140, 150, 170, 180.5) cm/ 31 (35, 41, 45, 49, 55, 59, 67, 71)", to be worn with 2.5–7.5 cm/1–3" positive ease

Yly has 79 cm/31" bust, stands 160 cm/5'3" tall, and is wearing a size 2.

Sara has 107 cm/42" bust, stands 163 cm/5'4" tall, and is wearing a size 4.

Yarn: Purl Soho Plein Air (DK weight; 67% merino wool, 33% organic cotton; 199 m/218 yds per 100-g/3.5-oz skein)

Shade: Chartreuse Pear; 2 (3, 3, 4, 4, 4, 5, 6, 6) skeins

OR

Ritual Dyes Undine DK (DK weight; 60% organic cotton, 40% linen; 250 m/273 yds per 100-g/ 3.5-oz skein)

Shade: Quartzite; 2 (2, 2, 3, 3, 3, 4, 5, 5) skeins

OR approx 368 (440, 489, 624, 678, 735, 901, 1006, 1049) m/402 (481, 535, 682, 742, 804, 985, 1100, 1147) yds of DK weight yarn

Gauge: 16 sts & 8 rows = 10 cm/4" in Cluster Pattern using US 7/4.5 mm hook, after blocking

Hook: US 7/4.5 mm

Always use a hook size that will result in the correct gauge after blocking.

Notions: Tapestry needle, locking stitch markers

note: Turn at the end of each row unless otherwise specified.

PATTERN

note: Front and Back pieces are identical. Front begins at left side of body. Back begins at right side of body. (The opposite applies for left-handed crocheters.) To create the neckline for this top, you will be working decreases and increases whilst also maintaining the lace pattern as established. This is a very useful skill indeed! Just follow the neckline instructions, and you'll see the shaping magically appear with minimal disruption to the pattern.

FRONT

first underarm

Ch40 (40, 40, 46, 46, 46, 52, 52, 52).

Set-up row (RS): 1dc in 4th ch from hook (missed 3-ch counts as dc throughout), 1dc in each ch to end. *38 (38, 38, 44, 44, 44, 50, 50, 50) sts*

Row 1 (WS): Ch3 (counts as first dc throughout), sk 1 st, 3dc in next st, [sk 2 sts, 3dc in next st] to last 2 sts, sk 1 st, 1dc in top of 3-ch.

Sizes 1 & 2 ONLY: Skip to First Strap.

Sizes 3, 4, 5, 6, 7, 8 & 9 ONLY

Row 2 (RS): Ch3, 1dc in each st to end.

Row 3 (WS): Ch3, sk 1 st, 3dc in next st, [sk 2 sts, 3dc in next st] to last 2 sts, sk 1 st, 1dc in top of 3-ch.

Sizes 3 & 4 ONLY: Skip to First Strap.

Sizes 5, 6, 7, 8 & 9 ONLY: Rep Rows 2 and 3 a further 1 (2, 2, 4, 5) times. Do not turn at the end of the last Row 3.

first strap

With WS facing, ch32 (35, 35, 38, 41, 41, 44, 47, 47), turn.

Next row (RS): 1dc in 4th ch from hook, 1dc in each ch and st to end. *68 (71, 71, 80, 83, 83, 92, 95, 95) sts*
Work Rows 1 and 2 of Cluster Pattern 4 (5, 5, 6, 6, 6, 7, 7, 7) times. *9 (11, 11, 13, 13, 13, 15, 15, 15) rows total on strap*

neck decreases

Row 1 (WS): Work in patt for 15 (15, 15, 16, 16, 16, 18, 19, 19) 3-dc clusters, sk 1 st, dc2tog, turn. *47 (47, 47, 50, 50, 50, 56, 59, 59) sts*

Row 2 (RS): Ch3, dc2tog, 1dc in each st to end. *46 (46, 46, 49, 49, 49, 55, 58, 58) sts*

Row 3: Work in patt for 14 (14, 14, 15, 15, 15, 17, 18, 18) 3-dc clusters, sk 1 st, 1dc, dc2tog. *45 (45, 45, 48, 48, 48, 54, 57, 57) sts*

Row 4: Ch3, dc2tog, 1dc in each st to end. *44 (44, 44, 47, 47, 47, 53, 56, 56) sts*

sizes 1 & 2 ONLY

Row 5 (WS): Work in cluster patt to end.
Skip to Neck Increases: ALL sizes again.

sizes 3 (4, 5) ONLY

Row 5 (WS): Work in patt for 13 (14, 14) clusters, sk 1 st, 2dc, dc2tog. *43 (46, 46) sts*

Row 6 (RS): Ch3, 1dc in each st to end.
Skip to Neck Increases.

sizes 6 (7, 8, 9) ONLY

Row 5 (WS): Work in patt for 14 (16, 17, 17) clusters, sk 1 st, 2dc, dc2tog. *46 (52, 55, 55) sts*

Row 6 (RS): Ch3, dc2tog, 1dc in each st to end. *45 (51, 54, 54) sts*

Row 7 (WS): Work in cluster patt to last 3 sts, sk 1 st, 1 dc, 1 dc in top of 3-ch.

neck increases

sizes 6 (7, 8, 9) ONLY

Row 1 (RS): Ch3, 1dc in same st, 1dc in each st to end. *46 (52, 55, 55) sts*

sizes 3 (4, 5, 6, 7, 8, 9) ONLY

Row 2 (WS): Work in patt for - (-, 13, 14, 14, 14, 16, 17, 17) clusters, sk 1 st, 2dc, 2dc in last st. - *(-, 44, 47, 47, 47, 53, 56, 56) sts*

ALL sizes again

Row 3 (RS): Ch3, 1dc in same st, 1dc in each st to end. *45 (45, 45, 48, 48, 48, 54, 57, 57) sts*

Row 4 (WS): Work in patt for 14 (14, 14, 15, 15, 15, 17, 18, 18) clusters, sk 1 st, 1dc, 2dc in last st. *46 (46, 46, 49, 49, 49, 55, 58, 58) sts*

Row 5: Ch3, 1dc in same st, 1dc in each st to end. *47 (47, 47, 50, 50, 50, 56, 59, 59) sts*

Row 6: Work in patt for 15 (15, 15, 16, 16, 16, 18, 19, 19) clusters, sk 1 st, 2dc in last st, do not turn, ch22 (25, 25, 31, 34, 34, 37, 37, 37). *65 (68, 68, 77, 80, 80, 89, 92, 92) sts*

Row 7 (RS): 1dc in 4th ch from hook, 1dc in each ch and st to end. *68 (71, 71, 80, 83, 83, 92, 95, 95) sts*

second strap

Work Rows 1 and 2 of Cluster Pattern 4 (5, 5, 6, 6, 6, 7, 7, 7) times. *9 (11, 11, 13, 13, 13, 15, 15, 15) rows total on Strap*

second underarm

Next row (WS): Work in patt for 12 (12, 12, 14, 14, 14, 16, 16, 16) 3-dc clusters, sk 1 st, 1dc in next st, turn. *38 (38, 38, 44, 44, 44, 50, 50, 50) sts*

Next row (RS): Ch3, 1dc in each st to end.

sizes 1 & 2 ONLY

Fasten off.

sizes 3 (4, 5, 6, 7, 8, 9) ONLY

Work Rows 1 and 2 of Cluster Pattern - (-, 1, 1, 2, 3, 3, 5, 6) times.

Fasten off.

BACK

Work as for Front.

FINISHING

Seam shoulders and sides. Weave in ends and block to measurements. Pink arrow shows direction the piece is worked.

a. Finished chest (fullest point) circumference: 80 (90, 105, 115, 125, 140, 150, 170, 180.5) cm/ 31½ (35½, 41¼, 45¼, 49¼, 55, 59, 67, 70¾)"

b. Body length (underarm to hem): 24 (24, 24, 27.5, 27.5, 27.5, 31.5, 31.5, 31.5) cm/9½ (9½, 9½, 10¾, 10¾, 10¾, 12½, 12½, 12½)"

c. Armhole depth: 19 (20.5, 20.5, 22.5, 24.5, 24.5, 26.5, 28.5, 28.5) cm/7½ (8¼, 8¼, 8¾, 9¾, 9¾, 10½, 11¼, 11¼)"

d. Strap width: 11.5 (14, 14, 16.5, 16.5, 16.5, 19, 19, 19) cm/4½ (5½, 5½, 6½, 6½, 6½, 7½, 7½, 7½)"

e. Neck width: 11.5 (11.5, 14, 14, 14, 16.5, 16.5, 16.5, 16.5) cm/4½ (4½, 5½, 5½, 5½, 6½, 6½, 6½, 6½)"

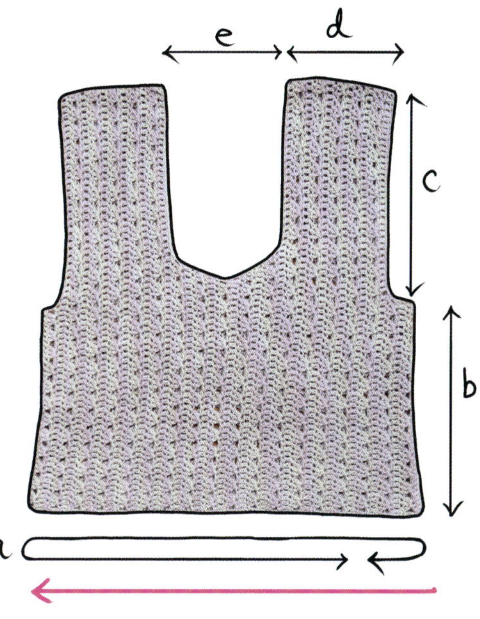

project 8

YLY

Granny Square Tee

project 8:

GRANNY SQUARE TEE

Now that you're a pro at granny squares, why not try something new with them? This cute tee uses a color change after the first round of each square, and you join the squares as you go to create the basic tee shape. You don't have to do the color change, of course, but we do love the way it creates a lovely pattern.

notes on construction:
Yly is worked in granny squares, which are joined together as you go. The front and back are worked separately, and once completed, the sides and underarms are seamed. Three further rows are worked on the front and back shoulders, and then the shoulders are seamed.

techniques you need to know:

- Chain (see page 12)
- Double crochet (see page 46)
- Granny square (see page 62)
- Mattress stitch seaming (see page 76)

techniques introduced:

- Joining granny squares as you go (see page 122–123)
- Creating a simple neck opening (see page 119)

note: If joining granny squares as you go feels too daunting at this stage, it's not essential. Simply complete the necessary number of squares in the usual way and seam them. Mattress stitch will give you a less stiff seam than a slip stitch seam, so we'd recommend that method if you decide to go this route.

pattern 8

YLY granny square tee

Sizes: 1 (2, 3, 4, 5, 6, 7, 8, 9)

Finished chest (fullest point) circumference: 76 (89, 101.5, 114.5, 127, 140, 152.5, 165, 178) cm/ 30 (35, 40, 45, 50, 55, 60, 65, 70)", to be worn with 7.5–15 cm/3–6" positive ease

Yly has 79 cm/31" bust, stands 160 cm/5'3" tall, and is wearing a size 2.

Yarn: Kelbourne Woolens Mojave (sport weight; 60% cotton, 40% linen; 169 m/185 yds per 50-g/ 1.75-oz skein)

Shades:

Yarn A: Electric Blue; 4 (4, 6, 7, 8, 8, 10, 12, 12) skeins

Yarn B: Flamingo Pink; 1 (1, 2, 2, 2, 2, 3, 3, 3) skeins

OR approx:

Yarn A: 620 (650, 860, 1045, 1240, 1335, 1565, 1885, 2000) m/680 (710, 940, 1140, 1355, 1460, 1710, 2190) yds of sport weight yarn

Yarn B: 145 (165, 215, 260, 310, 335, 390, 470, 500) m/160 (180, 235, 285, 340, 365, 425, 515, 545) yds of sport weight yarn

Gauge: 1 granny square = 6.5 cm/2½" square using US G-6/4 mm hook, after blocking

Hook: US G-6/4 mm

Always use a hook size that will result in the correct gauge after blocking.

Notions: Tapestry needle

top tip: weave in ends as you go

Going the two-color route? If you decide to make the center of your granny squares a different color from the rest of the square, as we have, you'll have quite a few yarn ends to deal with. Our suggestions?

1. Crochet over the tails with your new yarn. This simply means laying the yarn tail alongside the stitches you will be working into and crocheting over it so it is hidden.

2. Still have more tails? We recommend weaving those in after each square is complete. It is so much less daunting to sew those ends in little by little as opposed to having dozens (to put it lightly) once you've made the whole top.

PATTERN

FRONT

first granny square

**Using Yarn B, make magic ring.

Round 1: Ch3 (counts as first dc throughout), 2dc into magic ring, [ch3, 3dc into magic ring] 3 times, ch3, sl st in 3rd ch of beg 3-ch to join, pull tail firmly to close ring. *4 3-dc clusters, 4 3-ch sps*

Change to Yarn A.

Round 2: Ch3, 2dc into previous sp (at base of 3-ch), *ch1, (3dc, ch3, 3dc) into next 3-ch sp; rep from * twice more, ch1, 3dc into next 3-ch sp, ch3, sl st in 3rd ch of beg 3-ch to join. *8 3-dc clusters, 4 1-ch sps, 4 3-ch sps*

Round 3: Ch3, 2dc into previous sp, *ch1, 3dc into next 1-ch sp, ch1, (3dc, ch3, 3dc) into next 3-ch sp; rep from * twice more, ch1, 3dc into next 1-ch sp, ch1, 3dc into next 3-ch sp, ch3, sl st in 3rd ch of beg 3-ch. *12 3-dc clusters, 8 1-ch sps, 4 3-ch sps*

Fasten off.

Make another 47 (53, 71, 87, 103, 111, 131, 159, 169) squares, joining as you go (see pages 122–123) while working Round 3 of Granny Square, according to the diagram for your size on page 120. *48 (54, 72, 88, 104, 112, 132, 160, 170) granny squares total* **

left front shoulder

With RS of Front facing, join yarn to top-right corner.

Row 1: Ch3 (counts as first dc throughout), 1dc in same ch sp (at base of 3-ch), ch 1, (3dc, ch 1) in each 1-ch sp and corner join across 3.5 (4, 4.5, 5, 6, 6.5, 7, 7.5, 8) squares, ending with only 2dc in last ch sp or corner join, turn. You should have 10 (11, 13, 14, 17, 19, 20, 22, 24) 3dc clusters and 1 2dc cluster at each end. *12 (13, 15,16,19, 21, 24, 26) clusters total*

Row 2: Ch3, [3dc in next 1-ch sp, ch1] to last 1-ch sp, 3dc in last sp, 1dc in last st, turn.

Row 3: Ch3, 1dc in same st, ch1, [3dc in next 1-ch sp, ch1] to last st, 2dc in last st, turn.

right front shoulder

Beginning at top-left corner of Front, count 3.5 (4, 4.5, 5, 6, 6.5, 7, 7.5, 8) squares in toward center of body, join yarn in 1-ch sp or corner join.

Work Rows 1–3 as for Left Front Shoulder.

BACK

Work as for Front from ** to **.

back shoulders

With RS of Back facing, join yarn to top-right corner.

Row 1: Ch3 (counts as first dc throughout), 1dc in same ch sp (at base of 3-ch), ch1, (3dc, ch1) in each 1-ch sp and corner join across all upper back squares, ending with only 2dc in last corner sp, turn. You should have 28 (31, 34, 37, 46, 49, 52, 55, 58) 3 dc clusters, and 1 2dc cluster at each end. *30 (33, 36, 39, 48, 51, 54, 57, 60) clusters total*

Row 2: Ch4 (counts as 1dc and ch1), ch 1, [3dc in next 1-ch sp, ch 1] to end, 1dc in last dc, turn.

Row 3: Ch3, 1dc in same sp, ch 1, [3dc in next 1-ch sp, ch 1] to last ch sp, 2dc in last 1-ch sp, turn.

Fasten off.

FINISHING

Seam body sides, sleeve undersides, and shoulders using mattress stitch.

Weave in ends and block to measurements.

a. Chest circumference: 78 (91, 104, 117, 130, 143, 156, 169, 182)cm/30¾ (35¾, 41, 46, 51¼, 56¼, 61½, 66½, 71¾)"

b. Body length (hem to underarm): 19.5 (19.5, 19.5, 26, 26, 26, 32.5, 32.5, 32.5)cm/7¾ (7¾, 7¾, 10¼, 10¼, 10¼, 12¾ , 12¾, 12¾)"

c. Sleeve length: 13 (13, 13, 13, 19.5, 19.5, 19.5, 19.5, 19.5)cm / 5 (5, 5, 5, 7¾, 7¾, 7¾, 7¾, 7¾)"

d. Armhole depth: 21.5 (21.5, 28, 28, 28, 28, 28, 34, 34) cm/8½ (8½, 11, 11, 11, 11, 11, 13½, 13½)"

e. Neck width: 19 (19, 19, 19, 25.5, 25.5, 25.5, 25.5, 25.5) cm/7½ (7½, 7½, 7½, 10, 10, 10, 10, 10)"

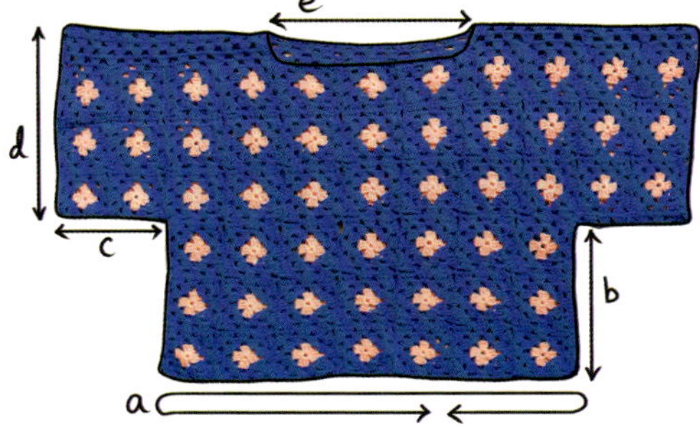

creating a simple neck opening

The drawings on the right show the difference between the extra rows added at the top of the front and back. The front has a gap in the middle which is your neck opening. The back doesn't have the gap as the rows are worked along the entire top.

yly top front

yly top back

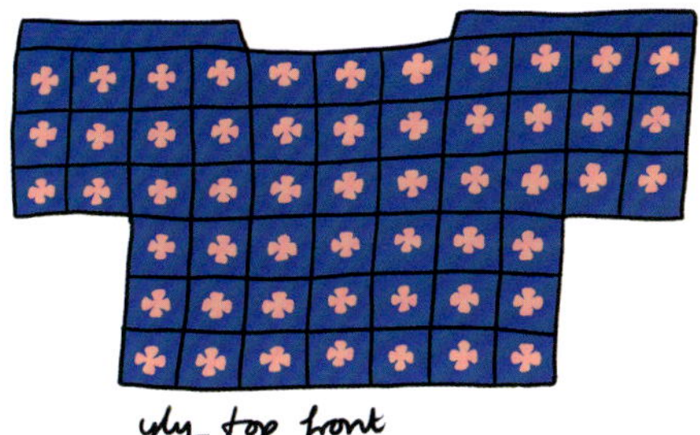

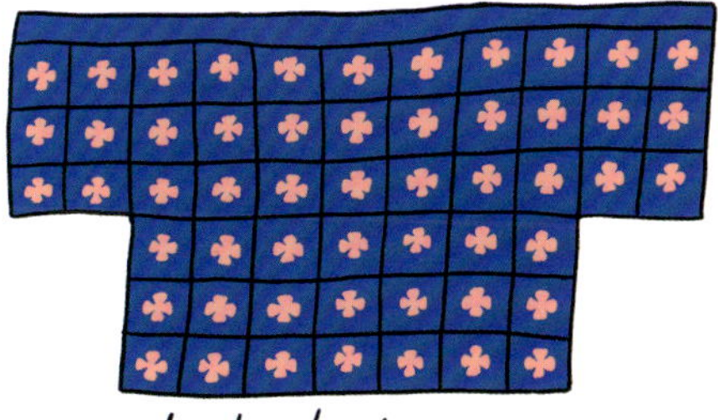

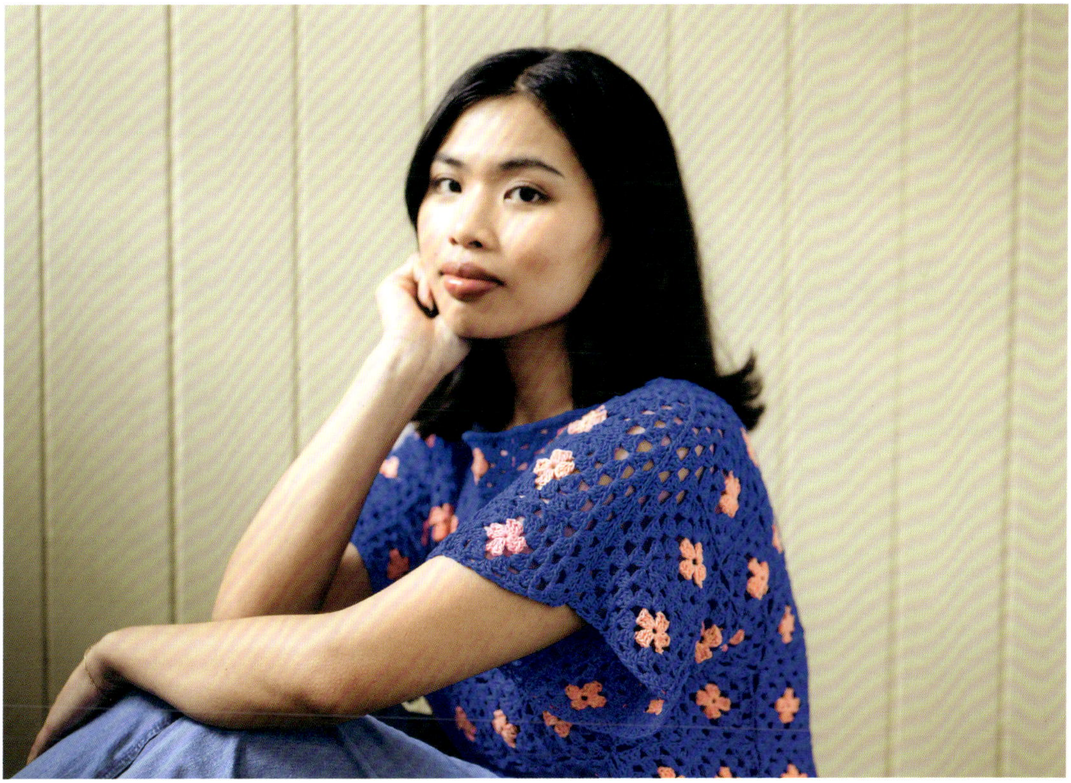

assembly diagrams

These diagrams show how you assemble your squares for the front and back of the top. The pink arrow shows the direction of assembly and the numbers show the order in which the rows of squares should be joined. But as long as you end up with the squares in the configuration shown for your size then the top will work!

The blue lines at the top show where the front shoulder stitches will be worked.

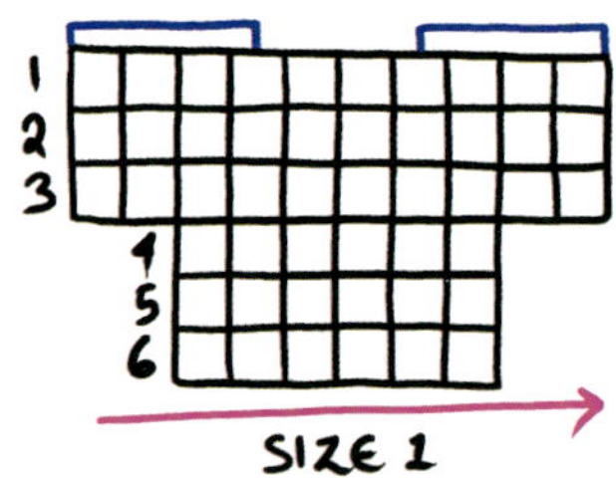

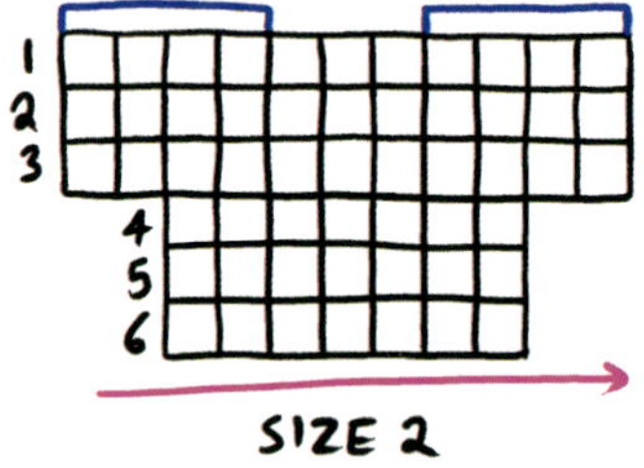

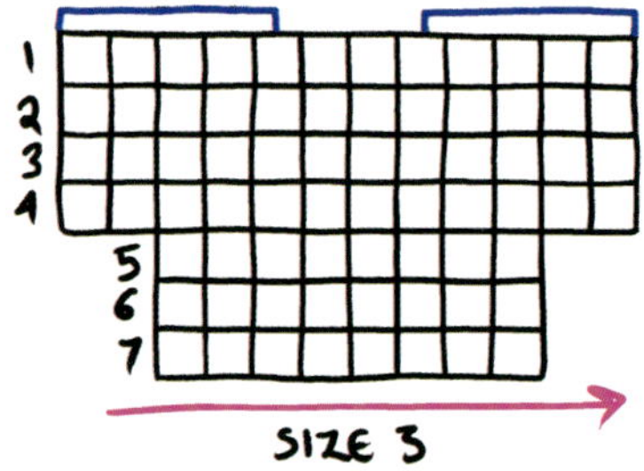

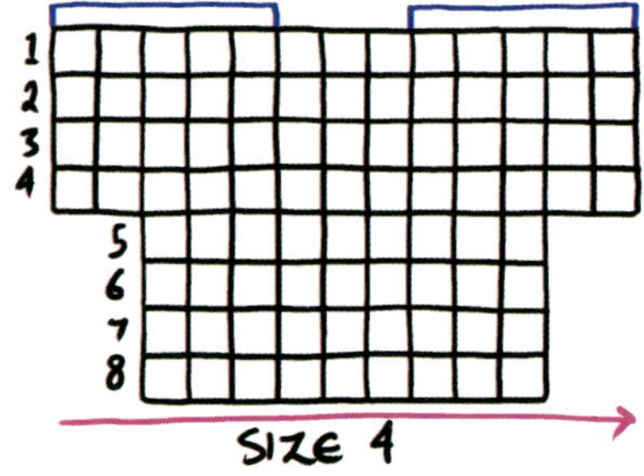

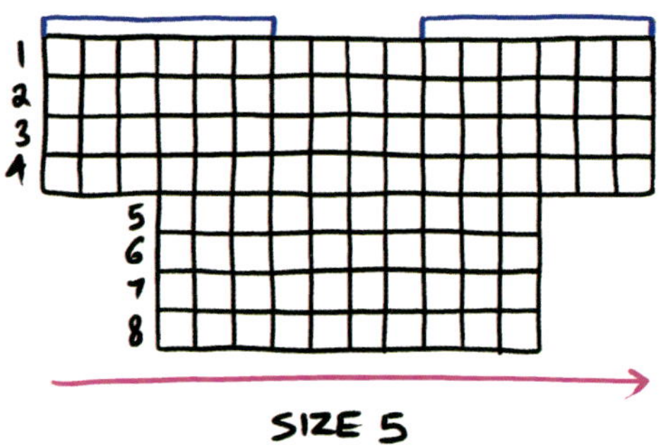

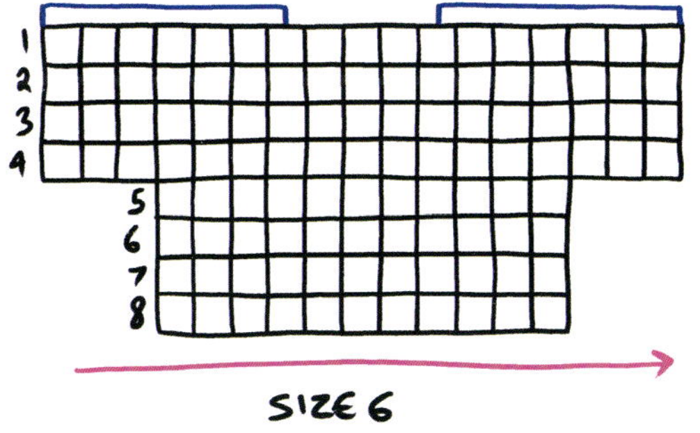
1
2
3
4
5
6
7
8
SIZE 6

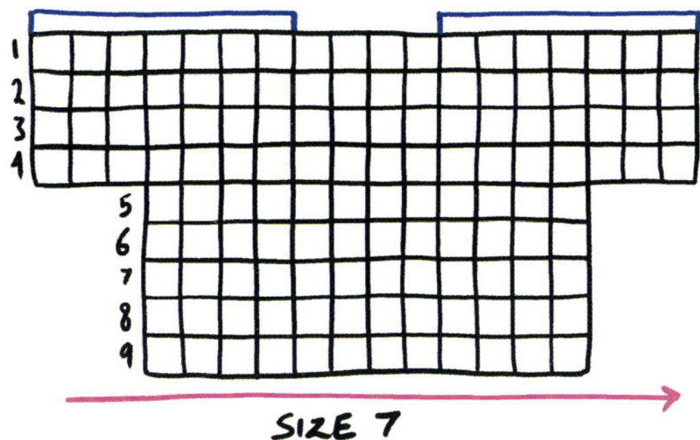
1
2
3
4
5
6
7
8
9
SIZE 7

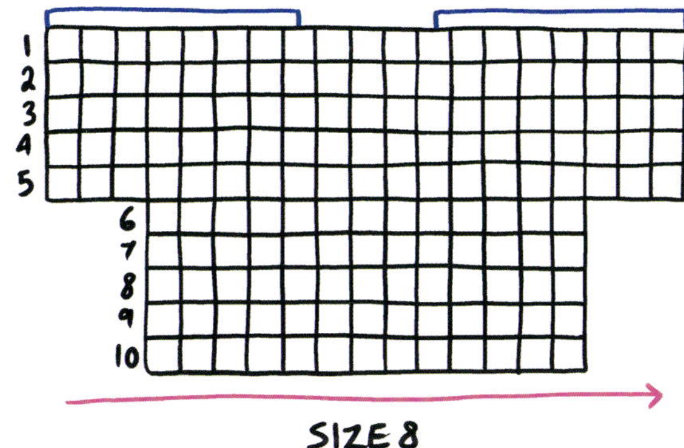
1
2
3
4
5
6
7
8
9
10
SIZE 8

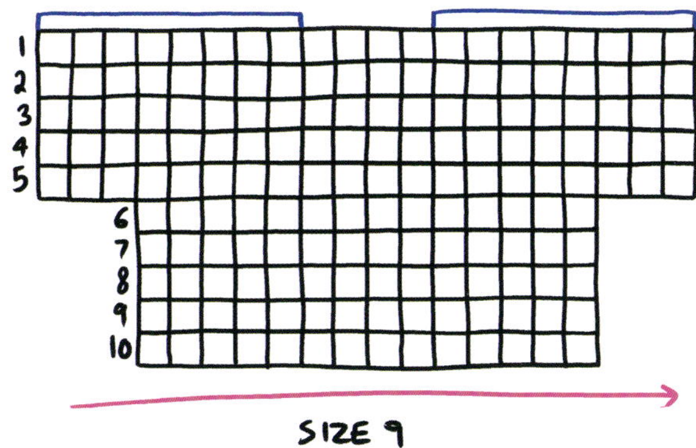
1
2
3
4
5
6
7
8
9
10
SIZE 9

joining granny squares as you go—two squares

"Join as you go" means you won't have to seam your squares when you are finished! You will join squares at chain spaces using a slip stitch. This tutorial shows joining squares along one side.

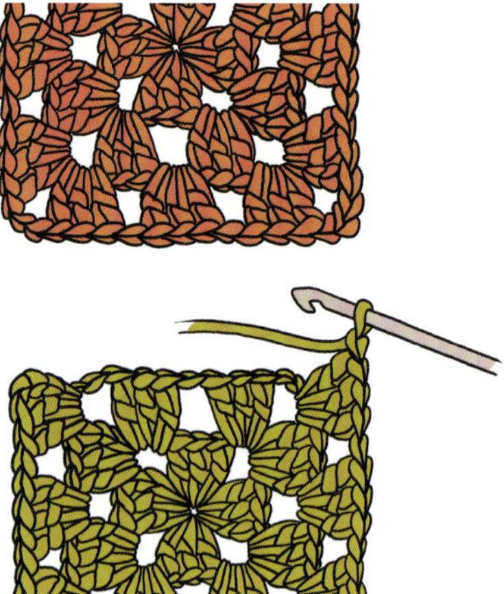

1. Make one square and fasten off (first square shown in orange). Make your second square, shown in yellow, stopping at the third corner after your first double crochet cluster, and chain 1. Line up the two squares as shown.

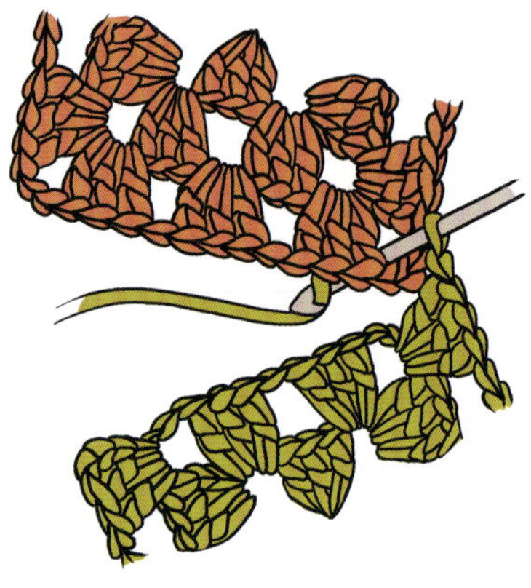

2. Insert your hook into the corresponding corner from front to back in your first square as shown and work a slip stitch.

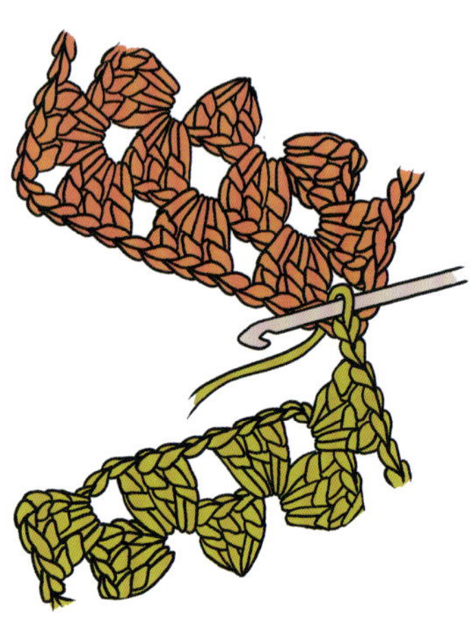

3. Slip stitch has been worked and the two squares should now be joined at the corner. This slip stitch counts as your second chain for the corner.

4. Work another chain stitch.

5. Complete your corner by working your second double crochet cluster.

6. Now insert your hook into the corresponding chain space in your first square, as shown.

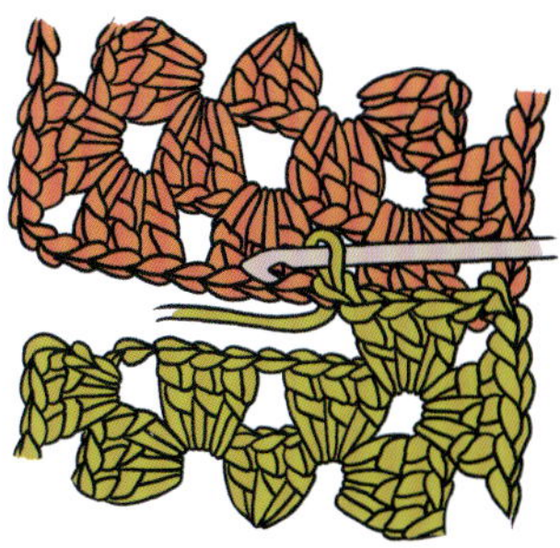

7. Now work a slip stitch through the chain space to join. This slip stitch is instead of the usual chain stitch.

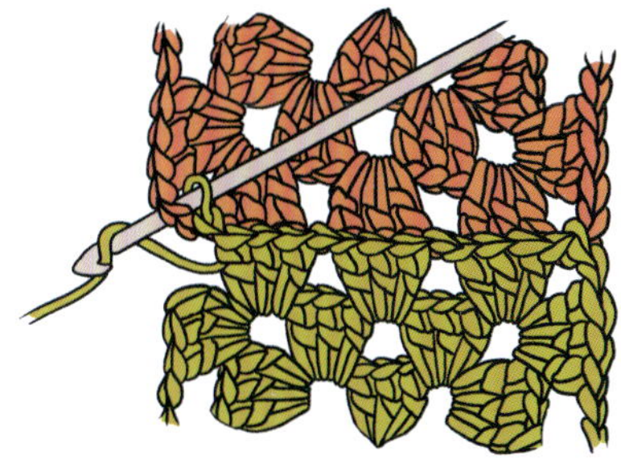

8. Work your next double crochet cluster and join to the next chain space in the same way (working a slip stitch through the corresponding chain space instead of the usual chain stitch). Then work the first double crochet cluster of the final corner. Chain 1, then work a slip stitch through the corner space.

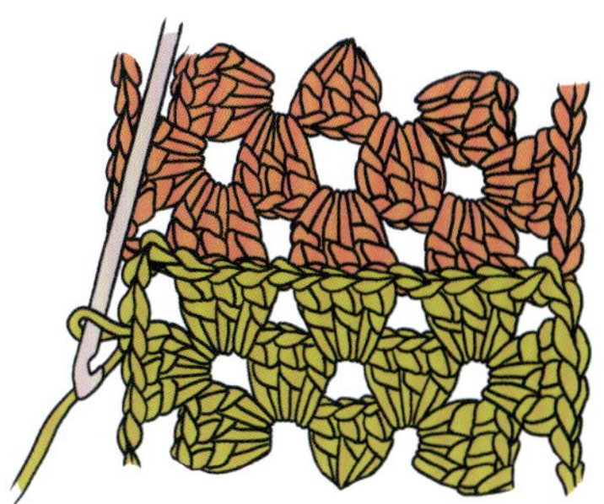

9. After completing your final corner join (you worked a chain stitch, then a slip stitch into the corner space, then a final chain stitch), join to the beginning of the round using a slip stitch to finish. The squares will be joined along one side.

joining granny squares as you go—joining into a corner

In order to make a lot of shapes (including the Yly top!), you will need to join squares along two sides. The principle is the same as with joining along one side only; you will be working slip stitches instead of chains into chain spaces.

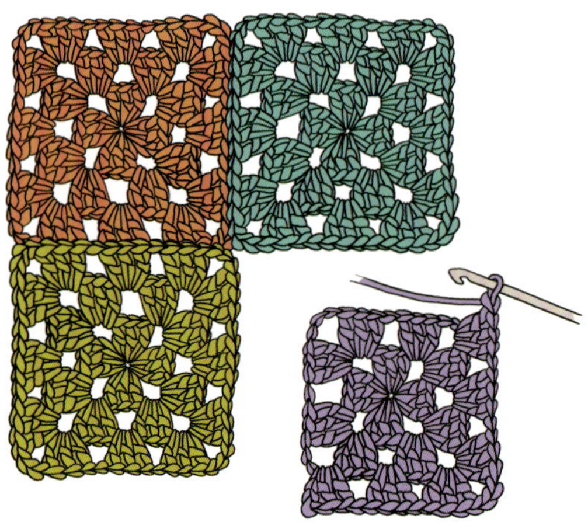

1. You will be joining a new square along two sides. The picture shows square one (orange), square two (yellow) and square three (blue) already joined. Work your next square, stopping at the third corner after working the first double crochet cluster and chain 1.

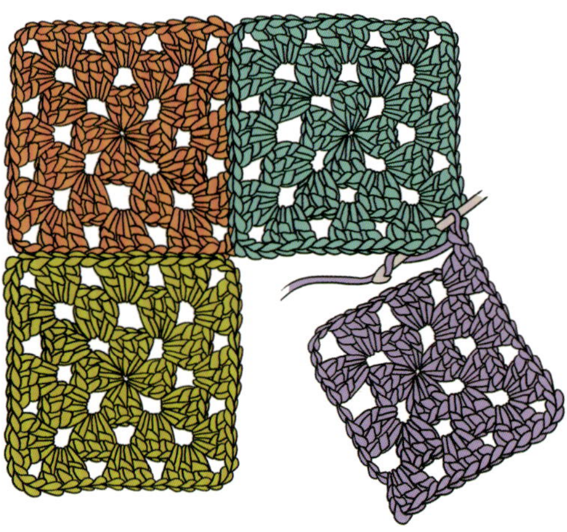

2. Join square four to square three by working a slip stitch through the corresponding corner space as shown.

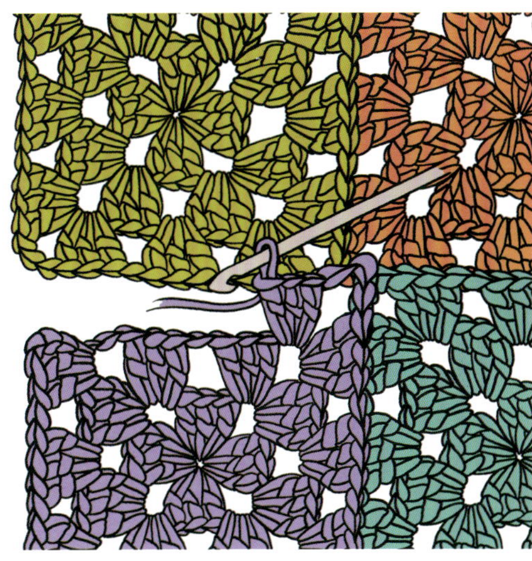

3. Continue to work that side, joining at the chain spaces using a slip stitch in place of a chain. When you get to the third corner, work your first double crochet cluster and chain 1, then slip stitch into the corner space of square one (orange), which is diagonally opposite. The bright yellow highlight shows the space you work into.

4. The squares have now been rotated 90 degrees clockwise. Finish your corner by working chain 1 and the second double crochet cluster. Now work the next double crochet cluster.

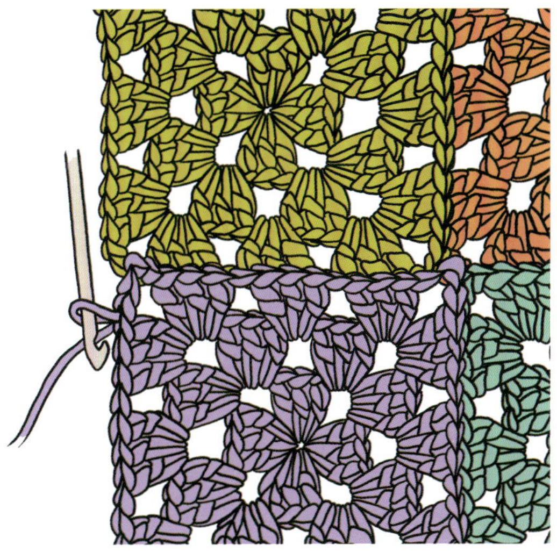

5. Work a slip stitch into the next chain space with your hook inserted as shown (as you have been doing!).

6. Continue the round, working slip stitches into the corresponding chain spaces in place of chain stitches, and join the corner as established by working a slip stitch into the corresponding space in place of the second chain stitch. Finish the square and fasten off.

project 9

ORILLIA

Granny-Inspired Pullover

project 9:
GRANNY-INSPIRED PULLOVER

This clever sweater uses the principles of increasing at the corners of a granny square and repurposes them as a raglan pullover. There are a few exciting new skills in this project—the decreases for the sleeves are worked in a clever way to maintain the granny stitch, and the ribbing is worked through the back loop of each stitch only (very easy and very effective). Although the fabric isn't solid, the fluffy yarn means it's still a warm sweater, and we are very excited about the opportunities to pair it with a long sleeve shirt in a fun color underneath.

notes on construction:
You start by working the neckline in the round, increasing at four "corners" until you have the yoke completed. This style of sweater construction is known as *raglan*. Once the upper body is worked, the front and back of the sweater are joined to form the lower body, which is worked downward to the hem. Sleeves are then added, working downward toward the wrist. The final flourish is the ribbing at the hems, which is worked at a right angle and joined to the pullover as you go.

techniques you need to know:
- Chain (see page 12)
- Single crochet (see page 15)
- Double crochet (see page 46)
- Working cluster stitches into a chain space (see page 50)
- Joining rounds using slip stitch (see page 66)

techniques introduced:
- Joining a chain to work in the round (see page 136)
- Decreasing in granny stitch pattern (see page 139)
- Ribbing working into the back loop only (see page 138)
- Working into both sides of a chain (see page 137)

pattern 9

ORILLIA granny-inspired pullover

Sizes: 1 (2, 3, 4, 5, 6, 7, 8, 9)

Finished chest (fullest point) circumference: 96.5 (112, 122, 132, 142, 157.5, 167.5, 178, 188) cm/ 38 (44, 48, 52, 56, 62, 66, 70, 74)", to be worn with 15.5–33 cm/6–13" positive ease

Yly has 79 cm/31" bust, stands 160 cm/5'3" tall, and is wearing a size 2.

Sara has 107 cm/42" bust, stands 163 cm/5'4" tall, and is wearing a size 3.

Yarn: Pom Pom x Hobbii Garland (worsted weight; 70% cotton, 30% alpaca; 105 m/114 yds per 50-g/ 1.75-oz ball)

Color-block version, shown in orange and peach (shown on opposite page):

Yarn A: Zinna 7 (8, 9, 10, 11, 13, 15, 16, 18) balls

Yarn B: Whim 4 (5, 5, 5, 6, 6, 6, 7, 7) balls

OR approximately

Yarn A: 640 (793, 917, 1035, 1155, 1355, 1501, 1654, 1818) m/695 (861, 996, 1124, 1254, 1471, 1630, 1795, 1973) yds of worsted weight yarn

Yarn B: 380 (441, 471, 520, 535, 592, 620, 656, 685) m/412 (479, 512, 564, 581, 642, 673, 712, 744) yds of worsted weight yarn

Contrast rib version, shown in beige and purple:

Yarn A: Chipmunk; 8 (10, 11, 13, 14, 16, 17, 19, 21) balls

Yarn B: Sylvie; 2 (2, 3, 3, 3, 3, 3, 3, 4) balls

OR approximately

Yarn A: 833 (1024, 1162, 1314, 1436, 1664, 1826, 1999, 2180) m/911 (1120, 1271, 1437, 1570, 1820, 1997, 2186, 2384) yds of worsted weight yarn

Yarn B: 188 (210, 227, 242, 255, 283, 296, 311, 324) m/204 (228, 246, 262, 276, 307, 321, 338, 352) yds of worsted weight yarn

Gauge: 16 sts & 8 rows = 10 cm/4" in granny cluster stitch using US H-8/5 mm hook, after blocking

note: Each 1-ch sp counts as 1 st when checking gauge.

Hooks: US H-8/5 mm

US 7/4.5 mm

US G-6/4 mm

Always use a hook size that will result in the correct gauge after blocking.

Notions: 6 locking stitch markers, tapestry needle

checking gauge

To check gauge, work a swatch as follows:

Using US H-8/5 mm hook, ch32.

Row 1: 2dc in 4th ch from hook (missed 3-ch counts as dc), *ch1, sk 3 ch, 3dc in next ch; rep from * 6 times, turn.

Row 2: Ch4 (counts as 1dc, 1 ch throughout), *3dc in next 1-ch sp, ch1; rep from * 6 times, dc in 3rd ch of turning ch, turn.

Row 3: Ch 3 (counts as dc), 2dc in first ch-1 sp, *ch1, 3dc in next 1-ch sp; rep from * 5 times, ch1, 2dc in last 1-ch sp, 1dc in 3rd ch of turning ch, turn.

Rows 4–15: Rep Rows 2 and 3 a further 6 times.

Fasten off and block.

PATTERN

yoke

Using largest hook and Yarn A, ch88 (104, 104, 104, 104, 120, 120, 120, 120). Being careful not to twist, sl st in first ch to join in round, place marker to indicate the beginning of the round.

Set-up round: Ch1 (does not count as a st), 1sc in each ch to end, sl st in first st to join. *88 (104, 104, 104, 104, 120, 120, 120, 120) sts*

note: From round 1 onward, the stitch counts are replaced with cluster counts for ease. So you will be counting 3dc clusters instead of each individual stitch to check your count (where appropriate!).

note: You may wish to mark each corner space with a locking stitch marker.

Round 1: Ch3 (counts as dc throughout), 2dc in same st (at base of 3-ch), [ch1, sk 3 sts, 3dc in next st] 8 (9, 9, 9, 9, 10, 10, 10, 10) times, ch1 (first corner), 3dc in same st, [ch1, sk 3 sts, 3dc in next st] 3 (4, 4, 4, 4, 5, 5, 5, 5) times, ch1 (second corner), 3dc in same st, [ch1, sk 3 sts, 3dc in next st] 8 (9, 9, 9, 9, 10, 10, 10, 10) times, ch1 (third corner), 3dc in same st, [ch1, sk 3 sts, 3dc in next st] 3 (4, 4, 4, 4, 5, 5, 5, 5) times,

note: Final 3dc will be worked in same st as beg 3-ch.

ch1 (fourth corner), sl st in 3rd ch of beg 3-ch. *16 sts inc; 26 (30, 30, 30, 30, 34, 34, 34, 34) 3-dc clusters; 9 (10, 10, 10, 10, 11, 11, 11, 11) for each front/back; 4 (5, 5, 5, 5, 6, 6, 6, 6) for each sleeve*

Round 2 (inc): Ch3, 2dc in corner sp at base of 3-ch, *[ch1, 3dc in next 1-ch sp] to corner, ch1, (3dc, ch1, 3dc) in corner sp; rep from * twice, [ch1, 3dc in next 1-ch sp] to 4th corner, ch1, 3dc in corner sp, ch1, sl st in 3rd ch of beg 3-ch. *16 sts inc; 120 (136, 136, 136, 136, 152, 152, 152, 152) sts*

Rep Round 2 a further 9 (11, 13, 15, 17, 19, 21, 23, 25) times. *11 (13, 15, 17, 19, 21, 23, 25, 27) inc rounds total; 66 (78, 86, 94, 102, 114, 122, 130, 138) 3-dc clusters; 19 (22, 24, 26, 28, 31, 33, 35, 37) for each front/back; 14 (17, 19, 21, 23, 26, 28, 30, 32) for each sleeve*

divide sleeves and body

note: You will only be working into the body stitches in this round, you will come back to the sleeves later in the pattern. See drawings on the opposite page for a visual guide.

Next round: Ch4 (counts as dc and 1-ch), [3dc in next 1-ch sp, ch1] to first corner, fold work in half so that the two long edges of the rectangle are aligned with WS together: First corner should meet second corner, and third corner should meet fourth corner. With RS facing, overlap 1st corner over 2nd corner, 3dc into both overlapped corner sps at once, [ch1, 3dc in next 1-ch sp] to 3rd corner, ch1, overlap 4th corner over 3rd corner, 2dc into both overlapped corner sps at once, sl st in 3rd ch of beg 4-ch to join. *38 (44, 48, 52, 56, 62, 66, 70, 74) 3-dc clusters*

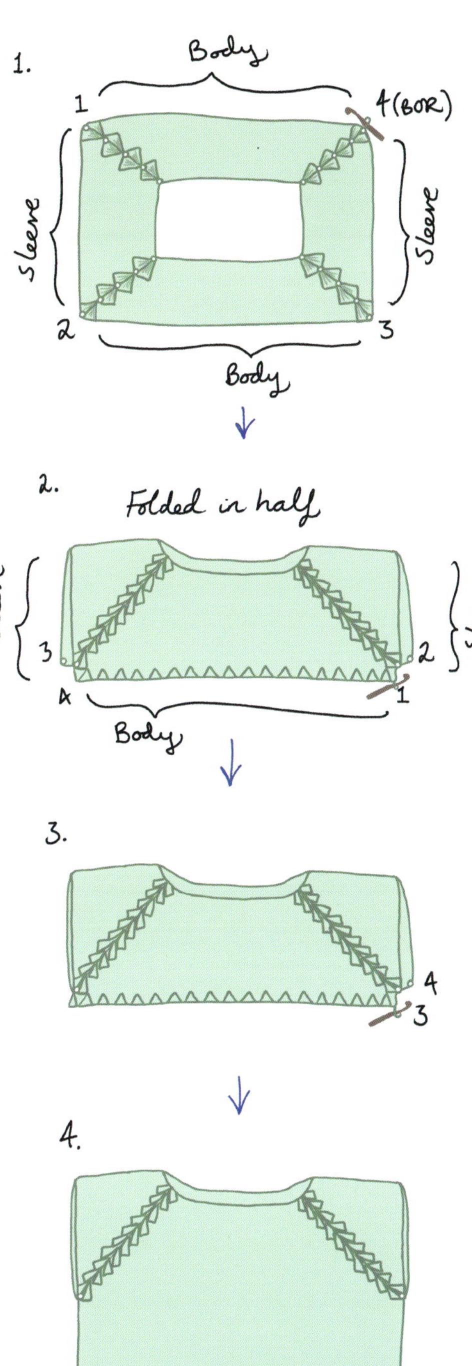

1. Here's how your work will look as you are working the yoke. The longer sides of the rectangle are body stitches and the shorter sides are your two sleeves.

2+3. When you come to divide for the body and sleeves you need to fold the rectangle in half as shown. You will be working through corners 1+2 at the same time, and through corners 3+4 at the same time. You don't need to work the sleeve stitches (you're going to come back to those later).

4. Here's how your sweater will look as you work the body, with length added only in the body section.

body

Round 1: Ch3, 2dc in 1-ch sp at base of 3-ch, [ch1, 3dc in next 1-ch sp] to end, ch1, sl st in 3rd ch of beg 3-ch.

Round 2: Ch4 (counts as dc and 1-ch), [3dc in next 1-ch sp, ch1] to last 1-ch sp (same sp as beg 3-ch), 2dc in last 1-ch sp, sl st in 3rd ch of beg 4-ch , sl st in next 1-ch sp.

Rep Rounds 1 and 2 until Body measures 23 cm/9" or desired length from underarm to beginning of split hem. If working color-block version, switch to yarn B after working 16.5 cm/6.5".

Next round: Ch1 (does not count as st), 1sc in each dc and 1-ch sp to end, sl st in first st to join and at the same time PM after 19 (22, 24, 26, 28, 31, 33, 35, 37) 3-dc clusters to indicate side of Body.

If using a contrast color for ribbing, fasten off.

front ribbing

note: Ribbing is worked perpendicularly to the Body and joined as you go.

Change to medium hook. If making contrast ribbing version, join Yarn B.

Row 1 (WS): Ch9, 1sc in 2nd ch from hook (missed ch does not count as a st), 7sc, sl st into next 2 sc from last body round, turn. *8 sc, 2 sl sts*

Row 2: Do not ch, sk 2 sl sts, 1sc in BLO of each sc to end, turn. *8 sc*

Row 3: Ch1 (does not count as st), 1sc in BLO of each st to end, sl st into next 2 sc from Body, turn. *8 sc, 2 sl sts*

Repeat Rows 2 and 3 until you have worked into the last sc for front, ending with Row 2.

Fasten off.

back ribbing

Continue with medium hook. If making contrast ribbing version, join Yarn B.

Row 1 (WS): Ch13, 1sc in 2nd ch from hook (missed ch does not count as st), 11sc, sl st into next 2 sc from last body round, turn. *12 sc, 2 sl sts*

Row 2: Do not ch, sk 2 sl sts, 1sc in BLO of each sc to end, turn. *12 sc*

Row 3: Ch1 (does not count as st), 1sc in BLO of each st to end, sl st into next 2 sc, turn. *12 sc, 2 sl sts*

Repeat Rows 2 and 3 until you have worked into the last sc for back, ending with Row 2.

Fasten off.

sleeves

If you are working the color-block version, switch to Yarn B after working 8".

Round 1: With largest hook, join Yarn A in any ch sp at back of Sleeve, approx halfway between shoulder and underarm, ch3 (counts as first dc throughout), 2dc in same st, [ch1, 3dc in next 1-ch sp] to end, ch1, sl st in 3rd ch of beg 3-ch. *14 (17, 19, 21, 23, 26, 28, 30, 32) 3-dc clusters*

Round 2: Ch4 (counts as dc and 1-ch throughout), [3dc in next 1-ch sp, ch1] to last 1-ch sp (same sp as beg 3-ch), 2dc in last 1-ch sp, sl st in 3rd ch of beg 4-ch, sl st in next 1-ch sp.

sleeve decreases

Place a locking stitch marker into the ch sp directly above the underarm cluster to mark decreases. Move locking marker up work as needed.

sizes 5 (6, 7, 8, 9) ONLY

Round 1: Ch3, 2dc in same st, ch1, [3dc in next 1-ch sp, ch1] to 2 ch sps before marked sp, 2dc in 1-ch sp, [ch1, 3dc in next 1-ch sp] 3 times, ch1, 2dc in next 1-ch sp, ch1, work in patt to end. *2 sts dec*

Round 2: Ch4, [3dc in next 1-ch sp, ch1] to first 2-dc cluster, sk 1-ch sp, 3dc in center of 2-dc cluster, sk 1-ch sp, [ch1, 3dc in next 1-ch sp] twice, ch1, sk 1-ch sp, 3dc in center of 2-dc cluster, sk 1-ch sp, ch1, [3dc in next 1-ch sp, ch1] to last 1-ch sp, 2dc in last 1-ch sp, sl st in 3rd ch of beg 4-ch. *6 sts dec*

Rep Rounds 1–2 a further 1 (2, 3, 4, 5) times. *19 (20, 20, 20, 20) 3-dc clusters*

ALL sizes

Round 1: Ch3, 2dc in same st, ch1, [3dc in next 1-ch sp, ch1] to marked sp, 2dc in marked 1-ch sp, ch1, [3dc in next 1-ch sp, ch1] to end, sl st in 3rd ch of beg 3-ch. *1 st dec*

Round 2: Ch4 (counts as dc and 1-ch), [3dc in next 1-ch sp, ch1] to 2-dc cluster, sk 1-ch sp, 3dc in center of 2-dc cluster, sk 1-ch sp, ch1, [3dc in next 1-ch sp, ch1] to last 1-ch sp, 2dc in last 1-ch sp, sl st in 3rd ch of beg 4-ch. *3 sts dec*

Work 5 (1, 1, 1, 1, 1, 1, 1, 1) rounds straight in patt.

Rep last 7 (3, 3, 3, 3, 3, 3, 3, 3) rounds a further 2 (5, 7, 8, 6, 6, 6, 5, 5) times. *11 (11, 11, 12, 12, 13, 13, 14, 14) 3-dc clusters*

Work straight in patt if necessary, until Sleeve measures 35 (35, 37.5, 39, 39, 39, 40, 40, 40) cm/ 13¾ (13¾, 14¾, 15¼, 15¼, 15¼, 15¾, 15¾, 15¾)" or 2.5 cm/1" less than desired length.

Next round: Ch1 (does not count as st), 1sc into each dc around (skipping all 1-ch sps), sl st in first st to join. *33 (33, 33, 36, 36, 39, 39, 42, 42) sts*

If using a contrast color for ribbing, fasten off.

cuff

note: Ribbing is worked perpendicularly to the Sleeve and joined as you go.

Change to medium hook. If making contrast ribbing version, join Yarn B.

Row 1 (WS): Ch5, 1sc in 2nd ch from hook (missed ch does not count as a st), 3sc, sl st into next 2 sc from last Sleeve round. *4 sc, 2 sl sts*

Row 2: Do not ch, sk 2 sl sts, 1sc in BLO of each sc to end, turn. *4 sc*

Row 3: Ch1 (does not count as st), 1sc in BLO of each st to end, sl st into next 2 sc, turn. *4 sc, 2 sl sts*

Repeat Rows 2 and 3 until you have worked into the last sc for Sleeve

note: You may only end with 1 sl st on final repeat for some sizes, ending with Row 2.

Join ends of ribbing using seaming method of choice.

Repeat for second Sleeve.

neckline

note: Neck ribbing is worked perpendicularly to the Body and joined as you go.

Using smallest hook, with RS facing, join Yarn B to neck edge.

Set-up round: Ch1 (does not count as st throughout), 1sc in each st around, sl st in first st to join, turn. *88 (104, 104, 104, 104, 120, 120, 120, 120) sts*

Row 1 (WS): Ch5, 1sc in 2nd ch from hook (missed ch does not count as st), 3sc, sl st into next 2 sc from last neck round. *4 sc, 2 sl sts*

Row 2: Do not ch, sk 2 sl sts, 1sc in BLO of each sc to end, turn. *4 sc*

Row 3: Ch1, 1sc in BLO of each st to end, sl st into next 2 sc, turn. *4 sc, 2 sl sts*

Repeat Rows 2 and 3 until you have worked into the last sc for neck. Join ends of ribbing using seaming method of choice.

FINISHING

Weave in ends and block to measurements.

a. Chest circumference: 96.5 (112, 122, 132, 142, 157.5, 167.5, 178, 188) cm/38 (44, 48, 52, 56, 62, 66, 70, 74)"

b. Yoke depth: 14 (16.5, 19, 21.5, 24, 26.5, 29, 31.5, 34.5) cm/5½ (6½, 7½, 8½, 9½, 10½, 11½, 12½, 13½)"

c. Body length (underarm to hem, front): 28 cm/11"

d. Sleeve length (underarm to cuff): 37.5 (37.5, 40, 41.5, 41.5, 41.5, 42.5, 42.5, 42.5) cm/14¾ (14¾, 15¾, 16¼, 16¼, 16¼, 16¾, 16¾, 16¾)"

e. Upper arm circumference: 35 (42, 47.5, 52.5, 57.5, 65, 70, 75, 80) cm/13¾ (16¾, 18¾, 20¾, 22¾, 25½, 27½, 39½, 31½)"

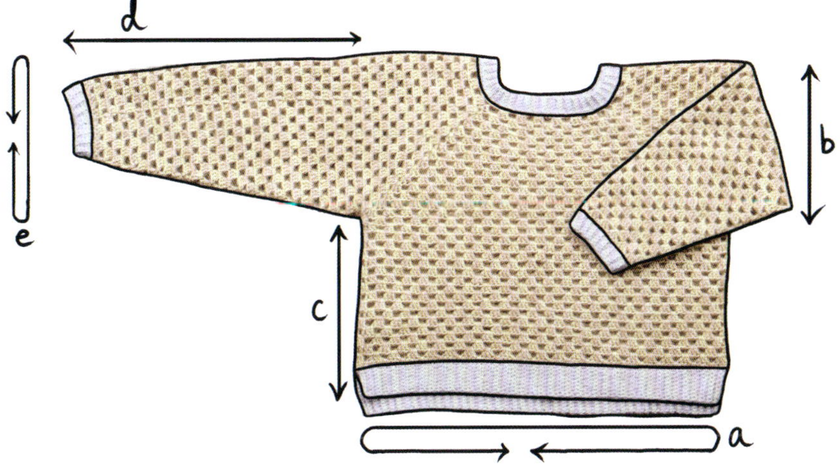

joining a chain to work in the round

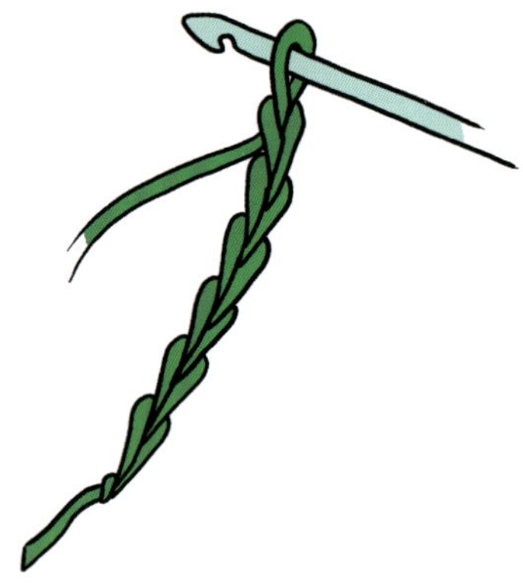

1. Work as many chain stitches as required by your pattern.

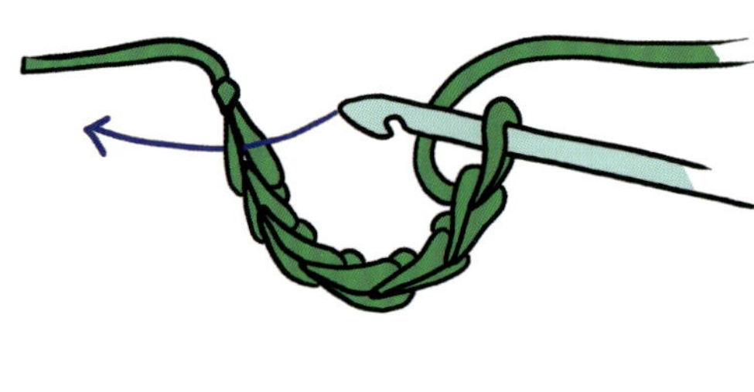

2. Now, being careful not to twist the chain, insert your hook into the first chain as shown.

3. Yarn over.

4. Pull the yarn over through the chain and then through the stitch on your hook. This slip stitch has joined the ends of the chain so it's a continuous circle.

5. You can now begin your first round. Here we are ready to work a round of single crochet, so one chain has been worked and you will begin your next stitch in the chain highlighted blue.

working into both sides of a chain

This tutorial shows single crochet stitches worked into both sides of a chain, but the principle is the same regardless of the kind of stitch you are making.

1. Make a slip knot and place it on your hook. With the original row of stitches worked into the chain upside down and right side facing, insert your hook into the "bottom" of the chain, following the path indicated by the arrow.

2. Begin to work your single crochet by pulling a loop through.

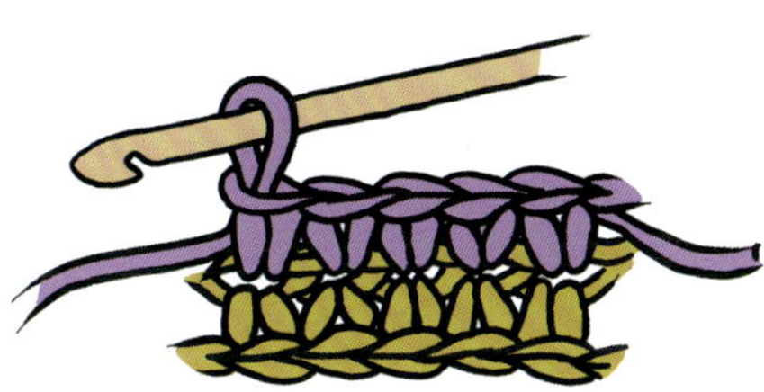

3. Complete your single crochet. You'll see that it sits almost like a mirror image of the stitch on the other side of the chain.

4. Continue working into the chain stitches as established.

ribbing—working into the back loop only (BLO)

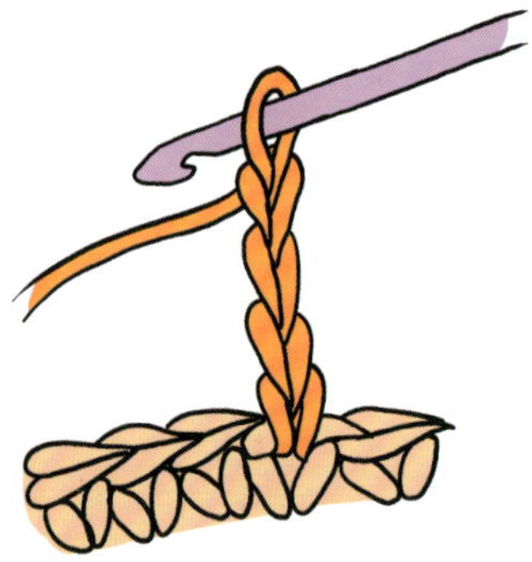

1. Begin your ribbing by working the number of chain stitches indicated in your pattern.

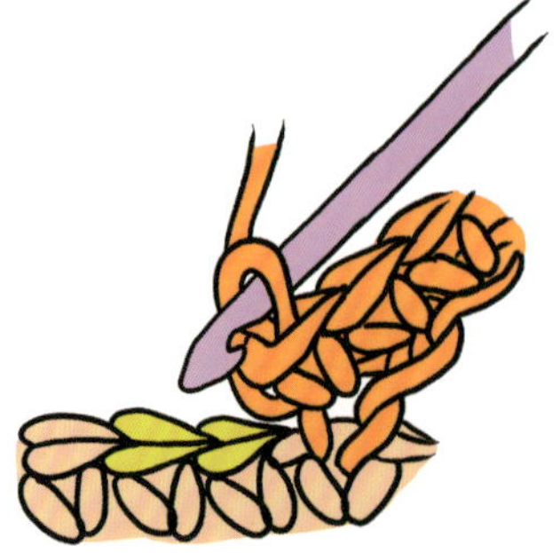

2. Now work your first row of single crochet stitches into that chain. You will reach the end of the row and be at a right angle to the main body of stitches as shown. Work a slip stitch into each of the next 2 stitches (highlighted in yellow) before you turn. This secures the ribbing to the main body of stitches as you go.

3. When your slip stitches are complete, turn to work back in the other direction.

4. You will now work back along your ribbing stitches, skipping the two slipped stitches. You will work in the back loop only (BLO). The back loop is the strand of the "V" that is farthest from you. Here you can see the back loop highlighted in red.

5. Here's a close-up to show the hook being inserted into the back loop only.

6. Working into the back loop only, continue to work as many single crochets as required. You will continue to work back and forth in rows, always working into the back loop and joining using slip stitches every other row. This will create a crochet ribbing.

decreasing in granny stitch

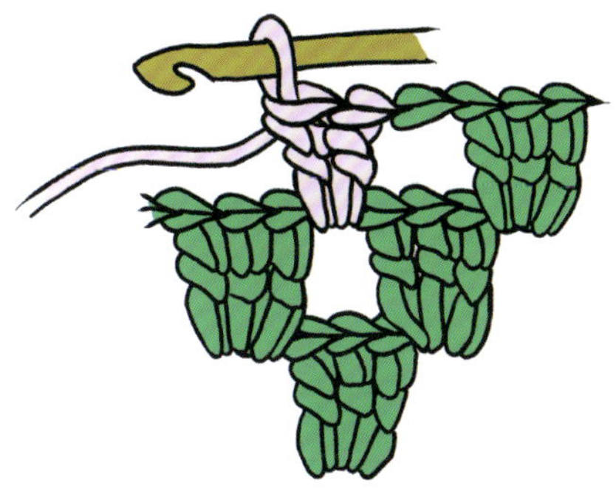

1. To begin your decrease, a 2dc cluster is worked in place of a 3dc one.

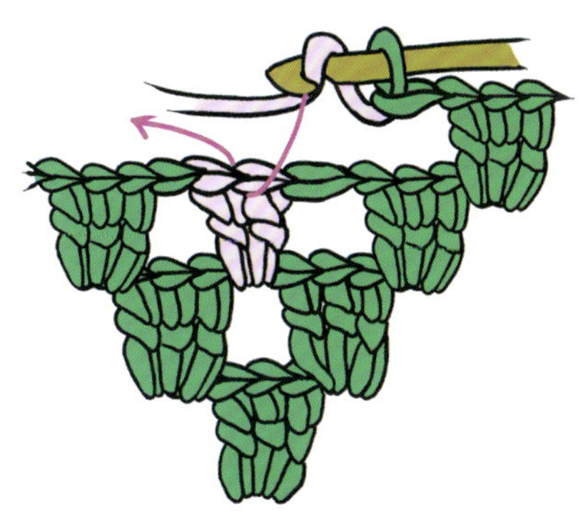

2. When you come to this 2dc cluster in your next round, skip the chain 1 space directly before it, and instead work a 3dc cluster in between the 2dc stitches, inserting your hook as shown.

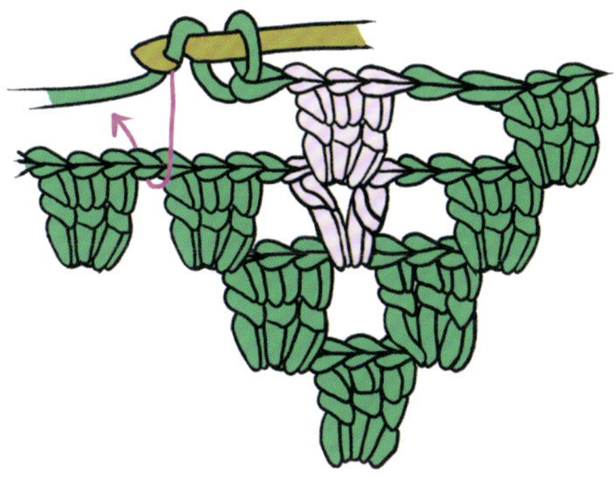

3. You then skip the chain space directly after the 2dc cluster and work your next 3dc cluster in the following chain space.

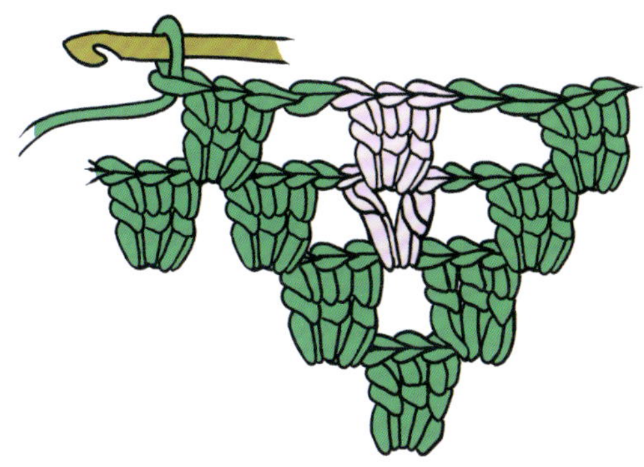

4. Here you can see the completed decrease.

project 10

ATWIN

Textured Cushion Cover

project 10:

TEXTURED CUSHION COVER

This cushion uses a more advanced stitch—the *interlocking block stitch*—to create a colorwork effect that will brighten any sofa or armchair, or it could even be a bed cushion. It doesn't mind where it lives. The stitch pattern is very fun once you get into the swing of it; we think your swatch will be a great place to practice it and also to try out fun color combos. The cushion shown is the larger size, but we have included options for smaller ones if you want a quicker project.

notes on construction:

The cushion is made in three pieces: one for the front, and two pieces for the back, which overlap to create an envelope style cover. Once all three pieces are finished, you work single crochet stitches through the layers to join them in your main color (MC). You can stop there if you choose, for a minimal edge, or work a picot edging like we have.

techniques you need to know:

- Chain (see page 12)
- Double crochet (see page 46)
- Changing color (see page 33)
- Slip stitch (see page 22)

Techniques Introduced:

- Fancy stitches: interlocking blocks (see page 148)
- Working with three colors (see note below)
- Picot edging (see page 150)
- Cushion construction (see page 151)
- Single crochet seam

note: This project alternates between three different colors, but that doesn't mean you need to cut and rejoin your yarns when changing shades. Simply drop the yarn you were using and pick up the color you need. This will save you a lot of time sewing in cut ends of yarn when you're finished. See the interlocking blocks tutorial on page 148 for more info!

pattern 10

ATWIN textured cushion cover

Sizes: 1 (2, 3)

Finished measurements before stuffing (without edging): 27 (35, 43.5) cm/10¾ (13¾, 17)" to fit a 30 (40, 50) cm/12 (16, 20)" square pillow form

Sample shown is size 3.

Yarn: De Rerum Natura Cyrano (heavy worsted weight; 100% wool; 150 m/164 yds per 100-g/3.5-oz ball)

Shades:

Yarn A: Genêt; 2 (2, 3) balls

Yarn B: Biche; 1 (2, 2) balls

Yarn C: Forêt; 1 (2, 2) balls

OR approx:

Yarn A: 158 (246, 326) m/173 (269, 356) yds of heavy worsted weight yarn

Yarn B: 113 (180, 263) m/123 (197, 287) yds of heavy worsted weight yarn

Yarn C: 113 (180, 263) m/123 (197, 287) yds of heavy worsted weight yarn

Gauge: 14.5 sts & 11.5 rows = 10 cm/4" in interlocking block stitch using US J-10/6 mm hook, after blocking

Hook: US J-10/6 mm

Always use a hook size that will result in the correct gauge after blocking.

Notions: 6 locking stitch markers, tapestry needle, cushion pad

note: Usually, the cushion pad needed for a cushion cover is 2.5–10 cm/1–4" larger than the finished size of the cover. For example, our size 3 cushion cover is 43.5 cm/17" square, and you would need a cushion pad approx 50 cm/20" square.

note: When checking gauge/stitch counts, each 1-ch sp counts as a st.

top tip: clip it good

You'll be sewing together multiple layers of fabric when assembling the cushion cover. To make this easier and keep everything in place, you can use quilt clips (clips that hold layers of fabric together when binding quilts). We love how these are purpose-made for the job, but really any clips will help, from clothes-pins to binder clips. Use whatever you have handy and thank yourself for making seaming that much more pleasant a task.

checking gauge

To check gauge, work a swatch as follows:

Using Yarn A, ch23.

Set-up row (RS): 1dc in 4th ch from hook (missed 3-ch counts as dc), 1dc in each of next 2 ch, [ch3, sk 3 ch, 1dc in each of next 3 ch] to end, do not turn, ch1 with Yarn B to change color, pull Yarn A tight but do not cut it, turn. *21 sts*

note: When working into sts from row below, work around the 3-ch above them.

Next row: *Ch3, sk 3 dc, [1dc into next skipped ch from row below] 3 times; rep from * to last 3 sts, ch3, sk next 2 dc, sl st in top of 3-ch, do not turn, ch1 with Yarn C to change color, pull Yarn B tight but do not cut it, turn.

Next row: Ch2 (counts as dc throughout), [1dc into next skipped st from row below] twice, *ch3, sk 3 dc, [1dc into next skipped st from row below] 3 times; rep from * to end, do not turn, ch1 with Yarn A to change color, pull Yarn C tight but do not cut it, turn.

Row 1 (WS): *Ch3, sk 3 dc, [1dc into next skipped st from row below] 3 times; rep from * to last 3 sts, ch3, sk next 2 dc, sl st in top of 2-ch, do not turn, ch1 with Yarn B to change color, pull Yarn A tight but do not cut it, turn.

Row 2: Ch2, [1dc into next skipped st from row below] twice, *ch3, sk 3 dc, [1dc into next skipped st from row below] 3 times; rep from * to end, do not turn, ch1 with Yarn C to change color, pull Yarn B tight but do not cut it, turn.

Repeat Rows 1 and 2, changing color as established (it will be clear which color is next as it will be the one a few rows below ready to be joined back in) until piece measures approx 12.5 cm/5", ending with Row 1.

Final row: Ch2, [1dc into next skipped st from row below] twice, *3sc, [1dc into next skipped st from row below] 3 times; rep from * to end.

Fasten off all colors and block.

PATTERN

front

**Using Yarn A, ch41 (53, 65).

Set-up row (RS): 1dc in 4th ch from hook (missed 3-ch counts as dc), 1dc in each of next 2 ch, [ch3, sk 3 ch, 1dc in each of next 3 ch] to end, do not turn, ch1 with Yarn B to change color, pull Yarn A tight but do not cut it, turn. *39 (51, 63) sts*

note: When working into sts from row below, work around the 3-ch above them.

Next row: *Ch3, sk 3 dc, [1dc into next skipped ch from row below] 3 times; rep from * to last 3 sts, ch3, sk next 2 dc, sl st in top of 3-ch, do not turn, ch1 with Yarn C to change color, pull Yarn B tight but do not cut it, turn.

Next row: Ch2 (counts as dc throughout), [1dc into next skipped st from row below] twice, *ch3, sk 3 dc, [1dc into next skipped st from row below] 3 times; rep from * to end, do not turn, ch1 with Yarn A to change color, pull Yarn C tight but do not cut it, turn.

Row 1 (WS): *Ch3, sk 3 dc, [1dc into next skipped st from row below] 3 times; rep from * to last 3 sts, ch3, sk next 2 dc, sl st in top of 2-ch, do not turn, ch1 with Yarn B to change color, pull Yarn A tight but do not cut it, turn.

Row 2: Ch2, [1dc into next skipped st from row below] twice, *ch3, sk 3 dc, [1dc into next skipped st from row below] 3 times; rep from * to end, do not turn, ch1 with Yarn C to change color, pull Yarn B tight but do not cut it, turn. **

Repeat Rows 1 and 2, changing color as set (it will be clear which color is next as it will be the one a few rows below ready to be joined back in) until piece measures approx 28 (37, 45) cm/11 (14½, 17¾)", ending with Row 1.

Final row: Ch2, [1dc into next skipped st from row below] twice, *3sc, sk 3 dc, [1dc into next skipped st from row below] 3 times; rep from * to end.

Fasten off all colors.

back (make two)

Work as for Front from ** to **, then repeat Rows 1 and 2, changing color as set (it will be clear which color is next as it will be the one a few rows below ready to be joined back in) until piece measures approx 20 (25.5, 30.5) cm/7¾ (10, 12)" ending with Row 2.

Final row: Using next color in sequence, ch1, then work 1sc into each dc on current row and 1dc into each skipped stitch from the row below.

Fasten off all colors.

join pieces together

Using the visual guide on page 151, with WS together and the two Back pieces overlapping at the center, lay Back pieces on top of Front piece, and join pieces as follows:

Round 1: Join Yarn A in any st along bottom edge and start to work sc around the entire edge through both pieces of fabric to join the pieces. When working through the top and bottom edges, line your sts up so that you work through the tops of corresponding sts. When working the sides, alternate between 2sc and 3sc per row end and working 3sc in each corner, working through both layers and being careful to line your sts up so that you work through the corresponding st on the Front and Back at the same time. End with a sl st in first st to join. The exact number of sts is not important, but ideally you should have the same number for each side, and end up with an even number overall.

Now begin your picot edging (if you are adding it, if not, fasten off) as follows:

Round 2 (Picot): [Ch3, sl st in FLO of same sc (at base of 3-ch), 2sc] to end, sl st in first st to join.

Fasten off.

FINISHING

Weave in ends and block to measurements. Insert your cushion pad.

Finished measurements before stuffing (without edging):
a. Length: 27 (35, 43.5) cm/10½ (13¾, 17)"
b. Width: 27 (35, 43.5) cm/10½ (13¾, 17)"
To fit a 30 (40, 50) cm/12 (16, 20)" square pillow form

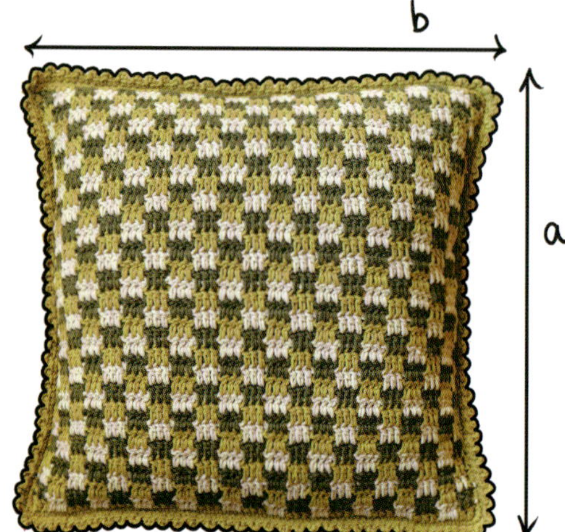

interlocking blocks

1. You have completed your foundation chain, worked 2 double crochet (3ch counts as first stitch), and 3 chain stitches. Skip 3 chain stitches and work your next double crochet into the fourth chain as shown.

2. Double crochet complete. There is a gap between the first set of double crochet stitches and the one just worked where you skipped stitches.

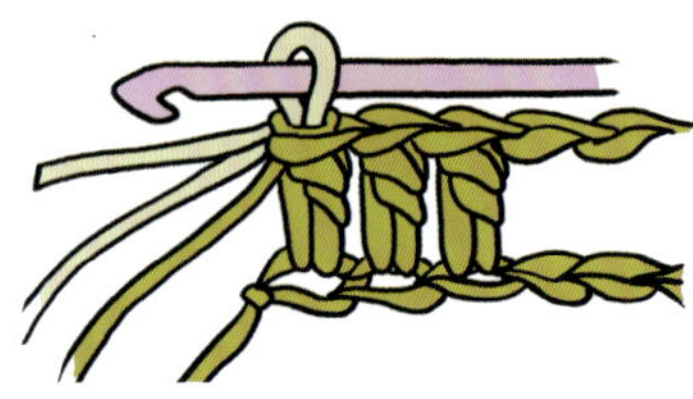

3. Work double crochet and chain repeats as instructed in your pattern. Finish your row with three double crochet. Now join Yarn B (cream) by dropping Yarn A (yellow) and pulling a loop through of Yarn B. Tighten Yarn A by pulling on it, but do not break it off. You'll be picking it up again soon.

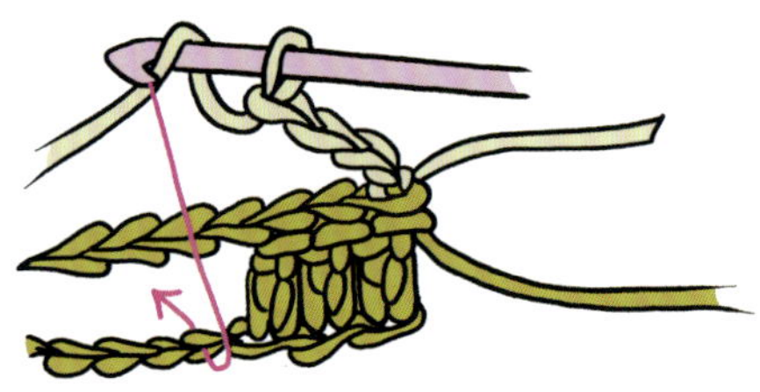

4. Turn and work 3 chain stitches. Now prepare to work a double crochet in the row below (which for this row is your foundation chain), your hook will follow the path shown.

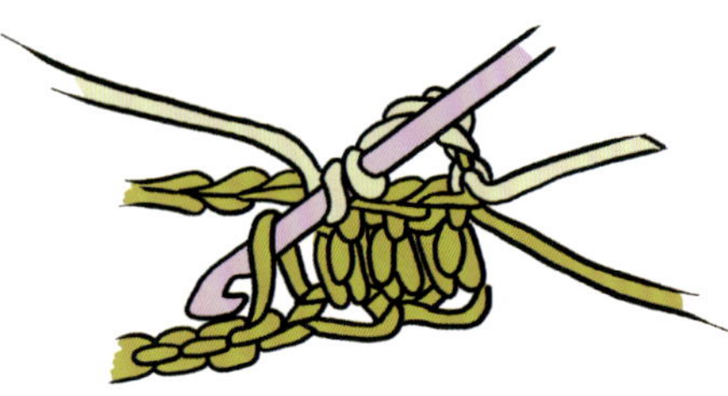

5. Insert the hook into the row below.

6. Continue working your double crochet around the chain stitches as shown by inserting the hook into the chain in the row below, and under the ch3 from front to back. Yarn over.

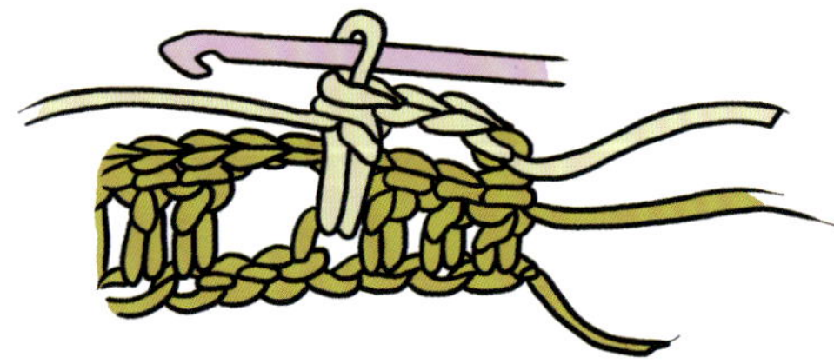

7. Complete your double crochet. It will sit around the chain stitches as shown.

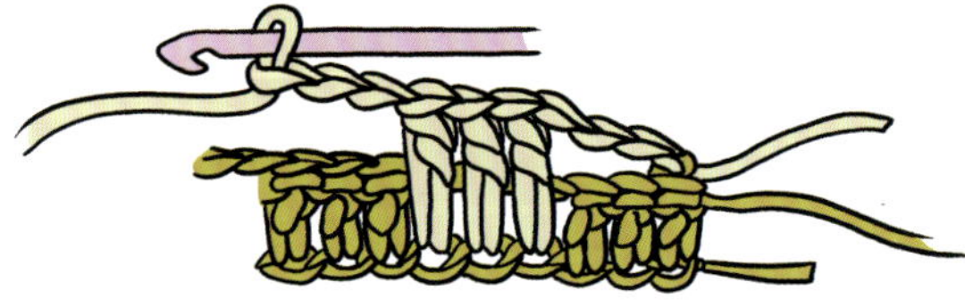

8. Complete the following two double crochets and 3 chain stitches.

9. When you reach the end of this row, you will join your final chain 3 to the double crochet of the row below with a slip stitch.

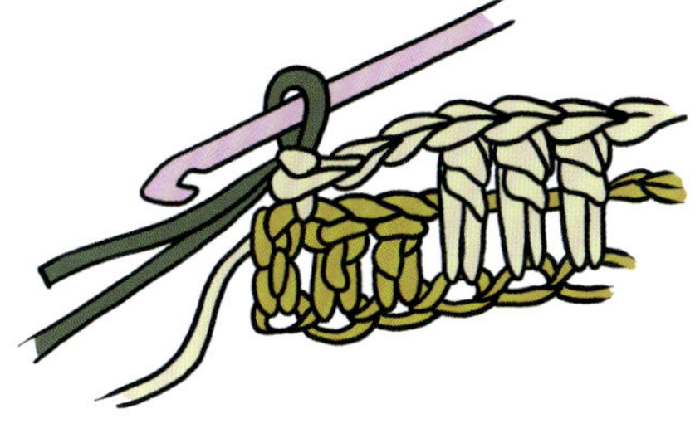

10. Drop Yarn B (cream) and join in Yarn C (green) in the same manner as you joined in the new yarn in Step 3.

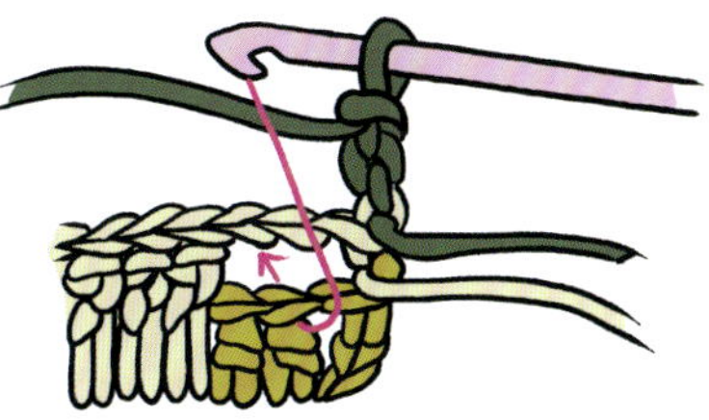

11. Chain 2 (counts as first double crochet) then work your next double crochet in the row below. From now on you will be working into the tops of the stitches in the row below. Your hook will follow the path shown.

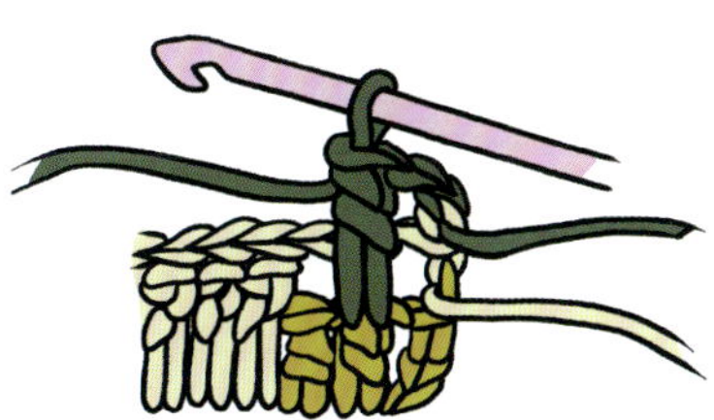

12. You have worked the double crochet in the row below.

13. Work another double crochet in the row below, chain 3, and then begin to work double crochet in the row below. The hook will follow the path shown.

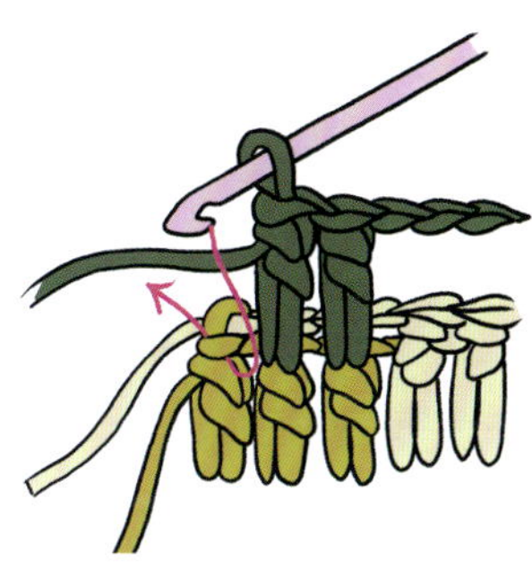

14. At the end of the row, work your final double crochet in the final double crochet from the row below. Don't worry about the extra color; you can work your stitch as normal.

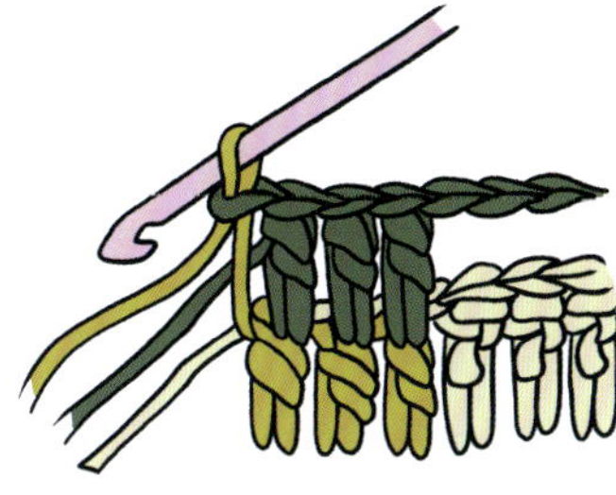

15. Now pick up Yarn A again and rejoin it in the same way you joined the other yarns. Make sure not to leave the strand running up the side too loose or pull it too tight. This strand will later be hidden by your cushion edging.

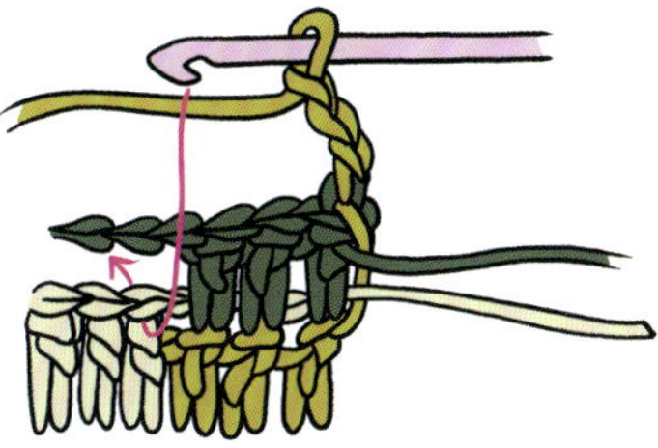

16. Turn and continue your row as instructed, working a ch3 to start. Follow your pattern instructions to continue working interlocking blocks. Make sure that when you pick up a color you don't pull it too tight or leave it too loose.

picot edging tutorial

1. Chain 3.

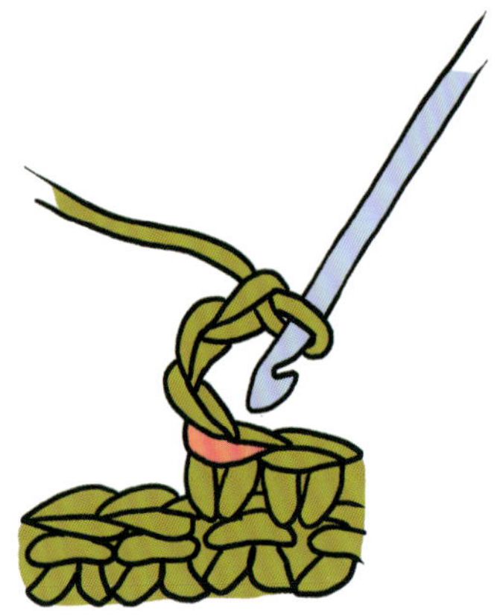

2. Insert your hook through the front loop only (FLO) of the last single crochet stitch you worked (at the base of your ch3). The loop you need to work through is highlighted in pink.

3. With the hook inserted, yarn over.

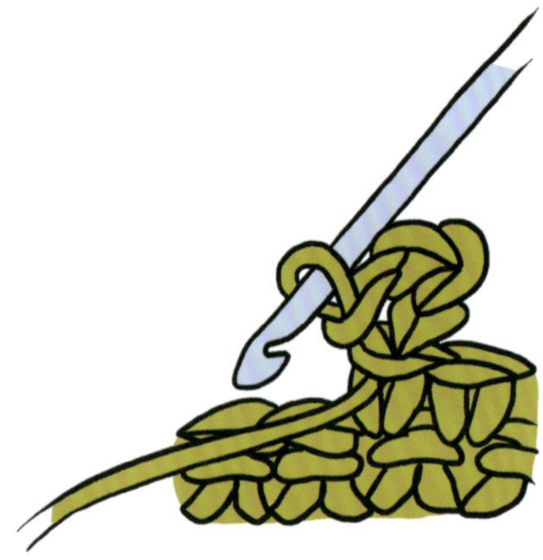

4. Pull yarn through both loops so that you've worked a slip stitch joining the ch3 back to the stitch below it. It will create a picot (which is like a little bobble).

cushion construction

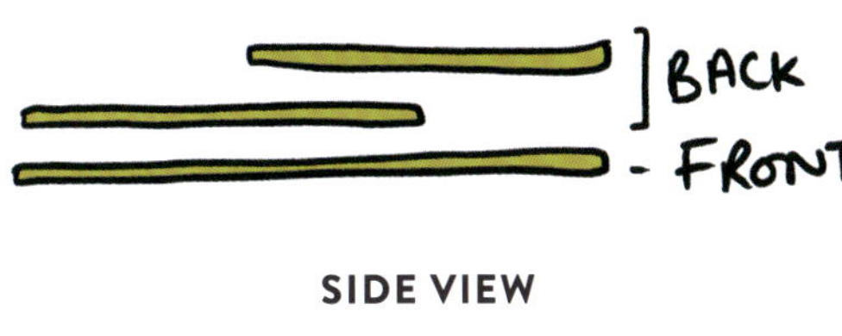

SIDE VIEW

1. When you complete crocheting your main pieces, you will have one larger front piece and 2 back pieces as shown.

2. Layer them with wrong sides together (right sides facing out), overlapping the back pieces in the middle as shown.

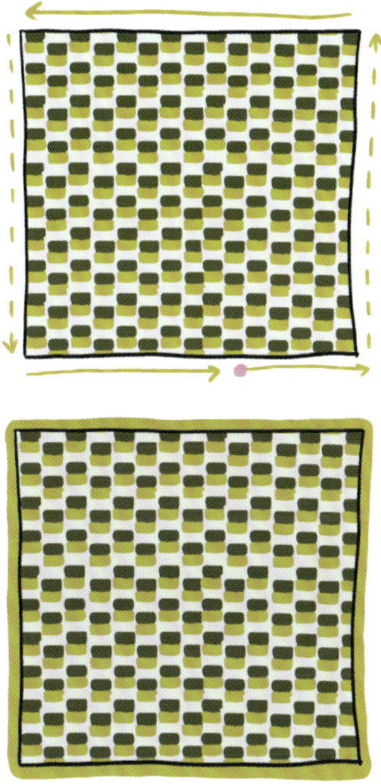

3. Rejoin your yarn (the pink dot indicates a good spot to do this!) and begin working through the layers to join, following the path of the arrows. The solid arrows show the top, where you can work through the tops of the stitches, and the bottom, where you can work into the other side of the chain. For these sides, you will be working a one-to-one ratio of stitches. The dotted lines show the sides where you will be working around the stitches themselves. We found alternating between two and three single crochets per row was a good way to get a good amount of stitches. Once you get back to where you started your join is complete!

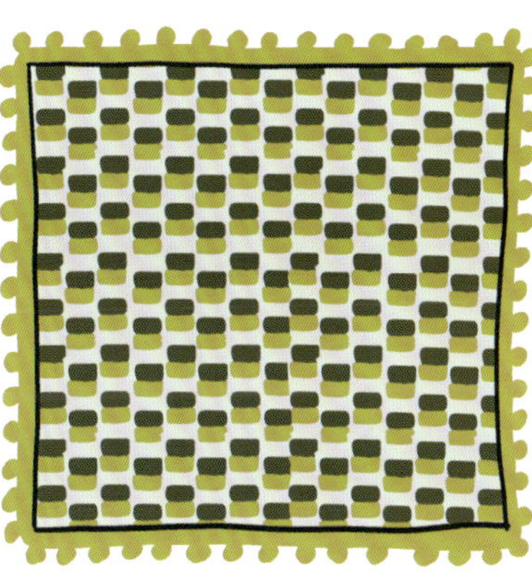

4. Work picot edging around the entire pillow, if desired.

project 11

QUINTE

House Slippers

project 11:

HOUSE SLIPPERS

We can't imagine a more heavenly feeling than padding around the house in squishy, cushy, hand-crocheted slippers. These slippers are a fun way to delve into the 3-D possibilities that crochet lends itself to. There are also a few new skills scattered around, so you can keep adding to your crochet (know) how. Once you've made yourself a pair, you won't be able to help making more for loved ones. What better way to show you care than an indulgent handmade gift meant for relaxing in?

We're introducing crochet chart reading with this pattern. Many crochet patterns use symbols instead of (or in addition to) written out row instructions. Once you get the hang of these, they will likely become your preferred way to work from a pattern. Just as with learning to read abbreviations, reading charts merely takes a little bit of practice. The chart symbols are really just an even more shorthand way of explaining how to make something, and we know that in no time you'll be a chart-reading pro. If you're still not convinced, never fear, the written instructions are included too.

notes on construction:

The slippers start with the sole, which is worked from the center out by working into both sides of a chain. Once the sole increases are completed, the sides of the slipper are worked, and then the first color is fastened off. The slipper top is worked separately and then joined to the bottom. Once joined, you continue around the rest of the slipper, working ribbing to create a cuff that can be doubled over when you finish so you have nice, cozy ankles.

techniques you need to know:

- Chain (see page 12)
- Single crochet (see page 15)
- Half double crochet (see page 61)
- Joining rounds with slip stitch (see page 66)
- Working through back loops only (see page 138)
- Working into both sides of a chain (see page 137)

techniques introduced:

- Measuring feet (see page 155)
- Following a chart (see page 160)
- Single crochet decreases (sc2tog) (see page 164)

note: If you branch out from the yarn we suggest in this pattern, you'll want to make sure it's a sturdy, not-too-soft yarn. The softer the yarn, and the more the fabric rubs against other surfaces (like the floor), the more prone your crocheted item is to pilling. There are many different types of fibers (that come from different breeds of sheep or other animals), and some are more rustic than others and can take a bit more wear and tear. Steer clear of merino or cashmere yarns for these, and veer toward a yarn that's a bit "crunchier," so to speak.

measuring feet

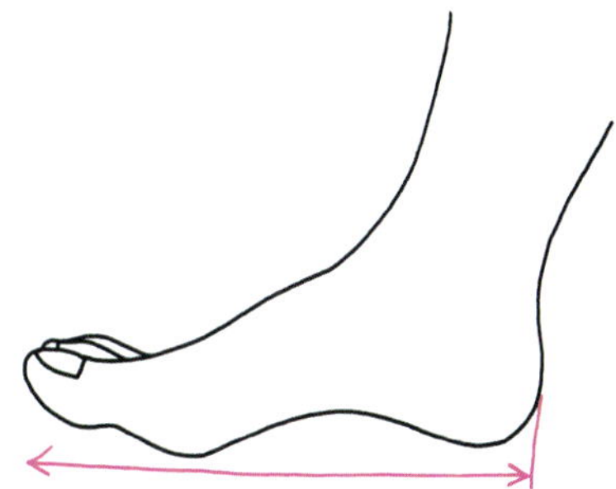

To work out the length of your foot, measure from your heel to the end of your longest toe.

top tip: adjusting the size of your slippers

The foot length of your slippers can be adjusted by working additional chain stitches when working the foundation chain of the sole. Each additional chain adds approximately 1 cm/⅜" to the final slipper length. The same number of additional chains must be added when working the foundation chain of the top of the slipper—for example, if the sole begins with ch24, the top of the slipper should begin with ch18.

The slipper can also be made deeper by adding further rounds of half double crochet where indicated in the pattern, to accommodate a wider foot. Remember that a larger slipper may require additional yarn.

pattern 11

QUINTE house slippers

Sizes: 1 (2,3,4)

To fit foot length: 23 (24, 25, 26) cm/9 (9½, 9¾, 10¼)", to be worn with approx 2.5 cm/1" ease

Finished dimensions: 20 (21.5, 22.5, 24) cm/7¾ (8½, 8¾, 9½)" long x 7.5 cm/3" wide at bottom of sole

note: Size is adjustable. See Top Tip on page 155.

Yarn: Rosa Pomar Cobertor (bulky weight; 100% Portuguese wool; 120 m/131 yds per 100-g/3.5-oz ball)

Shades:

Yarn A: Macela (802); 1 ball

Yarn B: Cinza (803); 1 ball

Also shown in shades Urze (806) and Tojo (808)

OR approx:

Yarn A: 48 (53, 58, 63) m/53 (58, 63, 69) yds of bulky weight yarn

Yarn B: 48 (53, 58, 63) m/53 (58, 63, 69) yds of bulky weight yarn

Gauge: 12 sts & 8 rows or rounds = 10 cm/4" in half double crochet using K-10.5/6.5 mm hook, after blocking

Hook: K-10.5/6.5 mm

Always use a hook size that will result in the correct gauge after blocking.

top tip!

Since these slippers are 3D, you will need to be a little more gentle when blocking them, and reshape them to dry. We would recommend a quick soak, being careful that the fabric doesn't get distorted, and then stuffing them with paper while they dry, like a pair of boots you got wet on a walk!

PATTERN

sole

note: You can follow either the chart for your size or the written instructions for rounds 1-3.

Using Yarn B, ch20 (21, 22, 23) or required number of chains (see Top Tip on page 155).

Round 1 (inc): 4hdc in 3rd ch from hook (missed 2-ch counts as hdc), 1hdc in each ch to last ch, 5hdc into last ch and PM in first of these 5 sts, do not turn but continue working along the other side of the chain, 1hdc in each ch to end, sl st in top of beg 2-ch to join. *42 (44, 46, 48) sts*

Round 2 (inc): Ch2 (counts as first hdc throughout), 1hdc into same st (at base of 2-ch), 1hdc, 3hdc in next st, 1hdc, 2hdc in next st, 1hdc in each st to marked st, 2hdc into marked st and replace marker in first of these 2 sts, 1hdc, 3hdc into next st, 1hdc, 2hdc into next st, 1hdc in each st to end, sl st in top of beg 2-ch. *50 (52, 54, 56) sts*

Round 3 (inc): Ch2, 1hdc into same st, [1hdc, 2hdc into next st] 4 times, 1hdc in each st to marked st, 2hdc into marked st, remove marker, [1hdc, 2hdc into next st] 4 times, 1hdc in each st to end, sl st in top of beg 2-ch. *60 (62, 64, 66) sts*

Round 4: Ch2, working in BLO, 1hdc in each st to end, sl st in top of beg 2-ch.

Round 5: Ch2, working in BLO again, 1hdc in each st to end, sl st in top of beg 2-ch.

note: For a deeper/roomier slipper, work additional reps of Round 5.

Round 6 (raising the heel): Ch1 (does not count as st), 1sc, 12hdc, 1sc in each st to end, sl st in first st to join.

Fasten off.

note: The hdc section of Round 6 is the heel end.

top of slipper

note: You can follow either the chart for your size or the written instructions for rows 1-3.

Using Yarn A, ch14 (15, 16, 17).

note: If additional chains were added to the Sole, remember to include them here as well (see Top Tip on page 155).

Row 1 (inc): 1hdc in 4th ch from hook (missed 3-ch counts as 1-ch and hdc), 1hdc in each ch to last ch, 5hdc into last ch and PM in last of these 5 sts, do not turn but continue working along the other side of the chain, 1hdc in each ch to end, ending with 1hdc in first ch of beg 3-ch, turn. *25 (27, 29, 31) sts*

Row 2 (inc): Ch2 (counts as first hdc throughout), 1hdc in each st to marked st, 2hdc into marked st, remove marker, 1hdc, 3hdc into next st, 1hdc, 2hdc into next st and PM in last of these 2 sts, 1hdc in each st to end, turn. *29 (31, 33, 35) sts*

Row 3 (inc): Ch2, 1hdc in each st to marked st, 2hdc into marked st, remove marker, [1hdc, 2hdc into next st] 4 times, PM in last st just worked, 1hdc in each st to end. *34 (36, 38, 40) sts*

Do not fasten off.

join top to bottom

With WS together, place the Top of Slipper piece on top of the Sole piece, aligning the toe sections (see diagram on page 165). With Top of Slipper facing up, beginning at right-hand corner and working through innermost loops only (one loop from each piece), work 1sc in each st around to join Top of Slipper to Sole. Once the top has been joined, continue working sc in innermost loop only of remaining sole sts and **at the same time** evenly dec 3 (3, 4, 5) sts, sl st in first st to join.

Do not fasten off, continue to work cuff as follows:

note: When working Row 1 along row ends of slipper top, treat each row end as 1 st.

Row 1: Ch11, 1sc in 2nd ch from hook (missed ch does not count as st), 9sc, sl st into next 2 sts of slipper top, turn.

Row 2: Sk 2 sl sts, 1sc in BLO of each st to end, turn. *10 sts*

Rep Rows 1 and 2 around the ankle opening.

Fasten off.

FINISHING

Seam ribbing using mattress stitch. Weave in ends and block to measurements.

a. Length: 20 (21.5, 22.5, 24) cm/7¾ (8½, 8¾, 9½)"
b. Width (at bottom of sole): 7.5 cm/3"
c. Depth (not including ribbing): 4 cm/1½"
d. Rib depth (folded): 4.5 cm/1¾"

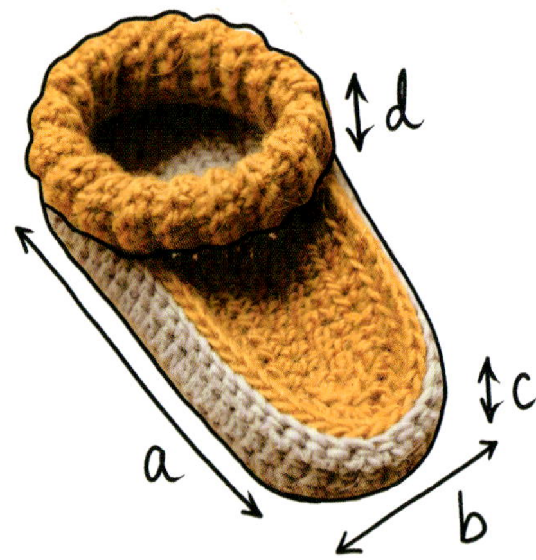

HOW TO READ A CROCHET CHART

A chart is just a visual representation of stitches, and many people find them easier to read than crochet instructions that are written out stitch by stitch. Each stitch used is given a symbol, and you work a stitch when you see its symbol in the chart. The symbols themselves look a bit like the stitches they make. The symbols will become second nature very quickly, just as abbreviations did.

Here you can see a key and a chart for the sole of the slipper pattern (shown in size 1). Note that the first chain stitch you will work is colored in red. The arrows show the direction you are working in when you work each round or row of the charts. (Note that if you are left-handed, it will be the opposite. See our digital version for lefties, link on page 14.) The chain is in pink, round/row 1 is in yellow, round/row 2 is in purple, and round/row 3 is in blue.

Stitches are worked into the stitch that they are positioned above. So where you can see two stitches positioned above one that's where you work two stitches into one, meaning that you increase! The number annotations shown correspond to which round you start with each turning chain (2 chains in this case because you are working half double crochet stitches). Charts are very clever because you can see how stitches work together before you've even made them!

In the photo at right, you can see just how much the chart for the top of the slipper looks like the actual stitches. Charts are a very handy visual reference.

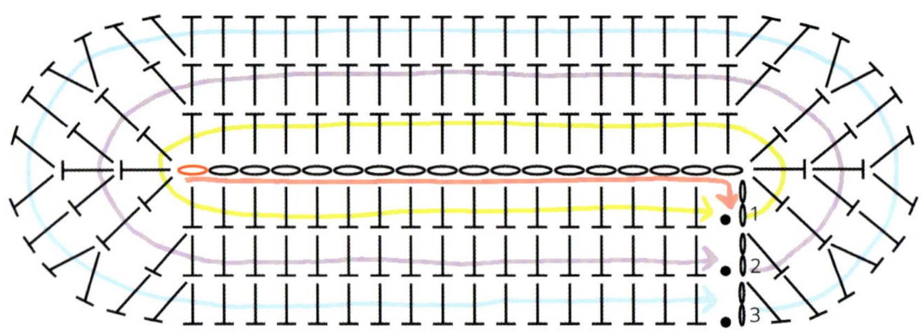

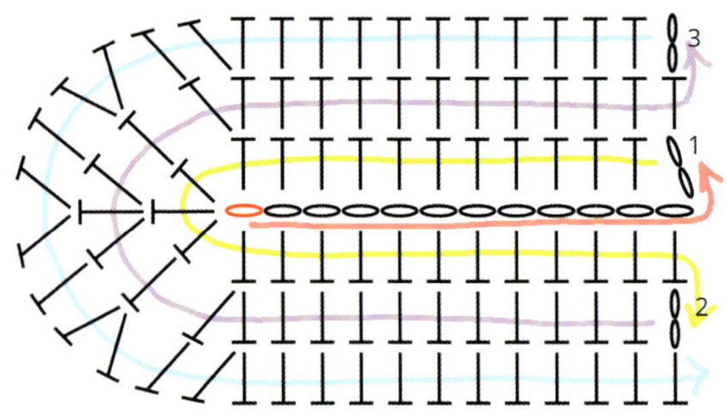

First Chain Stitch

Chain Stitch

● Slip Stitch

T Half Double Crochet

To help you come to grips with how charts work, here's how the sole chart corresponds to the written instructions, shown here in italics (remember this chart is for size 1 so it corresponds to those numbers).

Our extra notes are in ochre:

Using Yarn B, ch20 (21, 22, 23) or required number of chains (see Top Tip on page 155).

Notice that the last two chain stitches are shown here at a right angle, that's just to indicate that they are the first hdc of the following round.

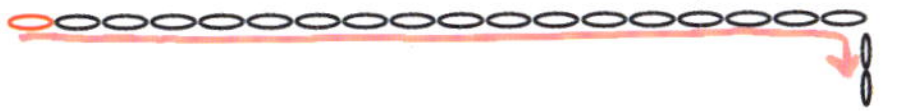

Round 1 (inc): 4hdc in 3rd ch from hook (missed 2-ch counts as hdc), 1hdc in each ch to last ch, 5hdc into last ch and PM in first of these 5 sts, do not turn but continue working along the other side of the chain, 1hdc in each ch to end, sl st in top of beg 2-ch to join. 42 (44, 46, 48) sts

Work counterclockwise from the two chain stitches that were at a right angle.

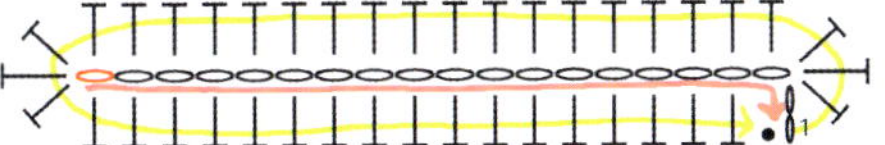

Round 2 (inc): Ch2 (counts as first hdc throughout), 1hdc into same st (at base of 2-ch), 1hdc, 3hdc in next st, 1hdc, 2hdc in next st, 1hdc in each st to marked st, 2hdc into marked st and replace marker in first of these 2 sts, 1hdc, 3hdc into next st, 1hdc, 2hdc into next st, 1hdc in each st to end, sl st in top of beg 2-ch. 50 (52, 54, 56) sts

Again, follow the chart counterclockwise beginning at where the previous round left off.

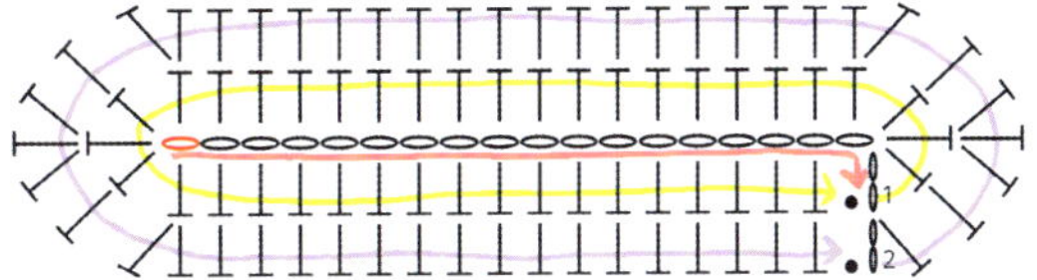

Round 3 (inc): Ch2, 1hdc into same st, [1hdc, 2hdc into next st] 4 times, 1hdc in each st to marked st, 2hdc into marked st, remove marker, [1hdc, 2hdc into next st] 4 times, 1hdc in each st to end, sl st in top of beg 2-ch. 60 (62, 64, 66) sts

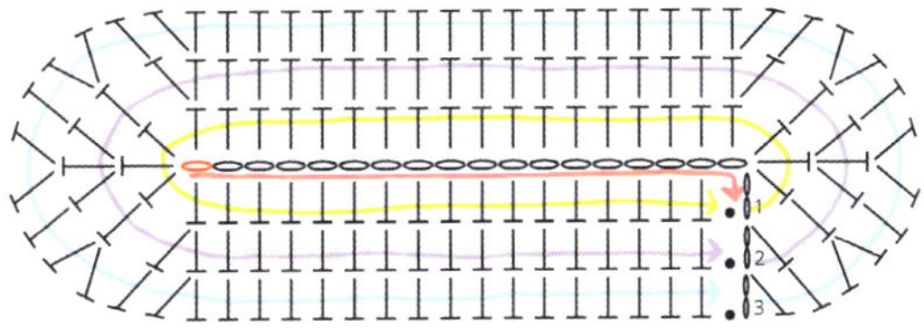

Ta-da! A whole slipper sole. As we said, a chart is basically a visual representation of the stitches. If it helps you to tape off the parts of a chart you aren't working in a particular round or row, go ahead! Just make sure you are using a tape that will come off easily such as a low tack masking tape or washi tape.

slipper charts

size 1

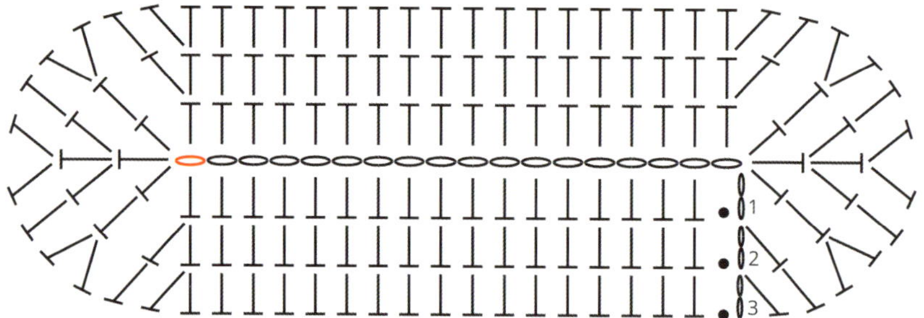

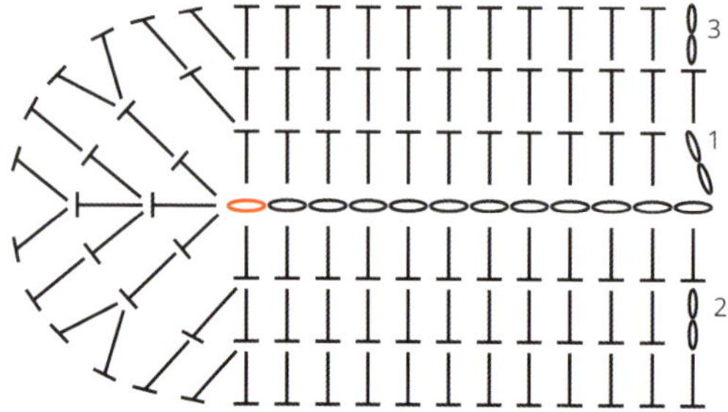

First Chain Stitch

Chain Stitch

Slip Stitch

Half Double Crochet

size 2

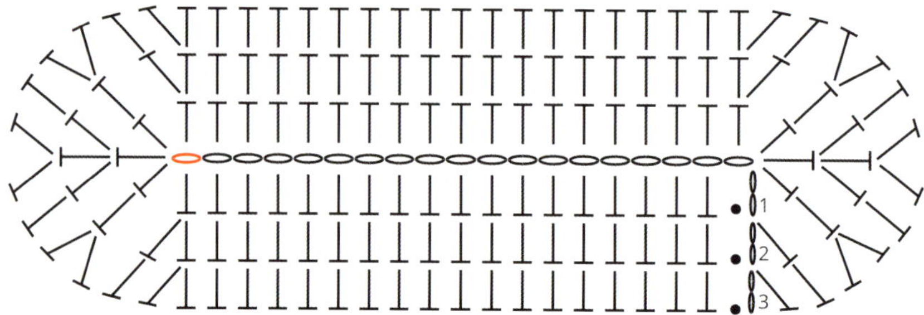

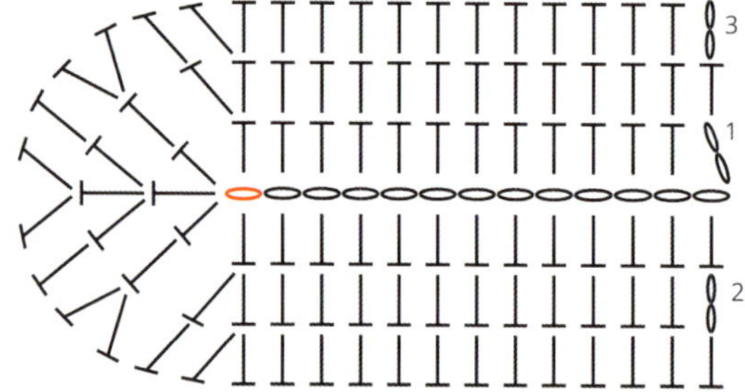

size 3

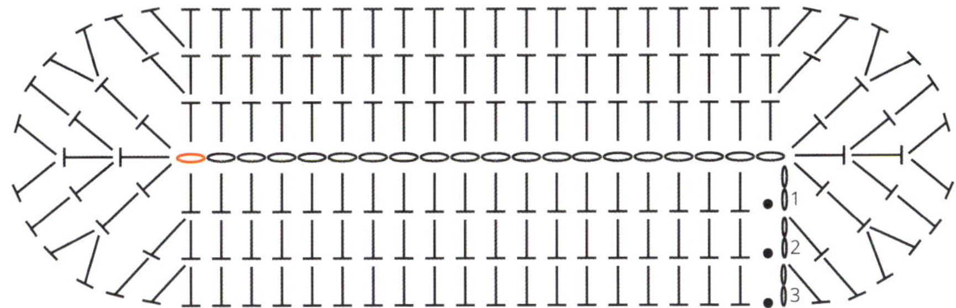

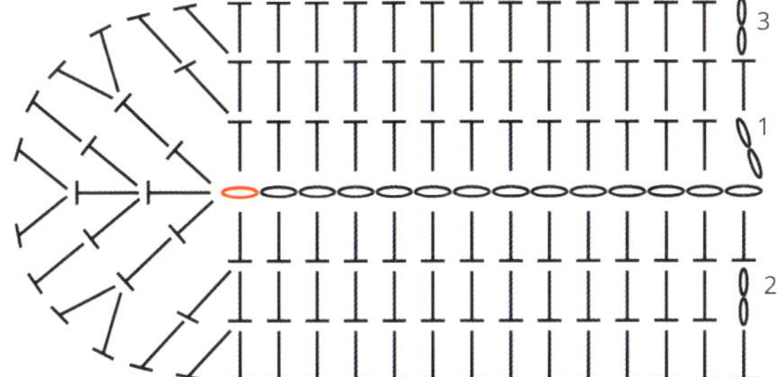

size 4

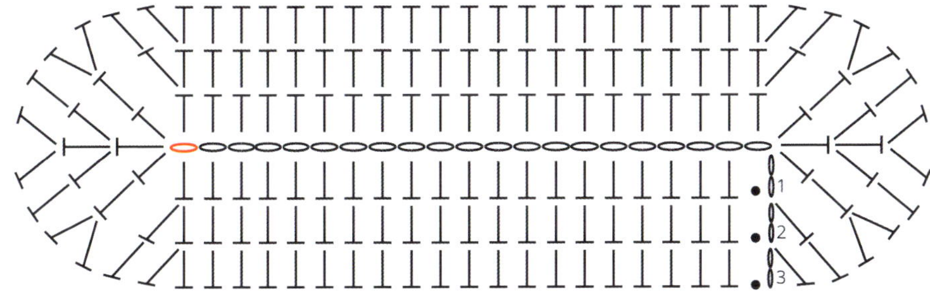

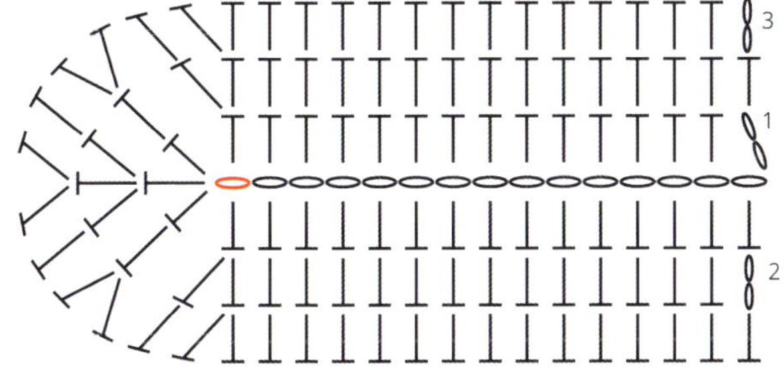

decrease—single crochet (sc2tog)

1. You will be working a decrease over the next two stitches (highlighted in light pink)

2. Insert your hook into the first stitch and pull a loop through.

3. Now rather than completing that single crochet, move on to the next stitch and pull a loop through. You will have three loops on your hook.

4. Yarn over and pull it through all three loops. You have decreased one stitch.

slipper assembly

1. You should have two pieces for your slipper, the sole and sides (referred to as the bottom), and the top.

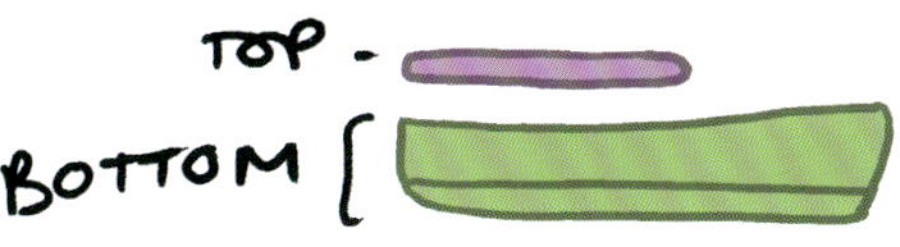

2. Lay the top over the toe end of the bottom as shown (making sure not to lay it on the higher heel section).

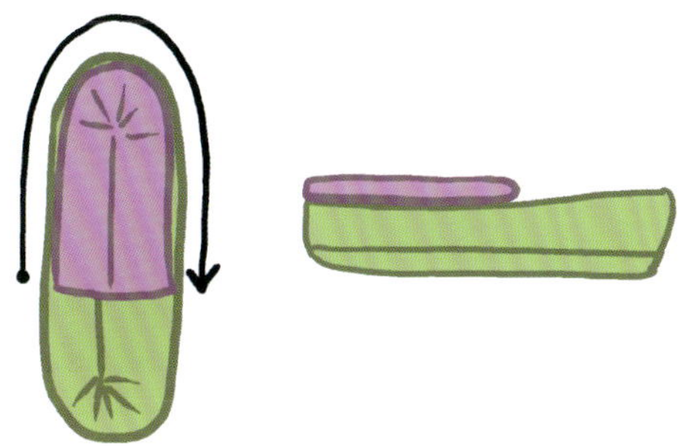

3. Work your join in the direction shown. The two pieces are now one.

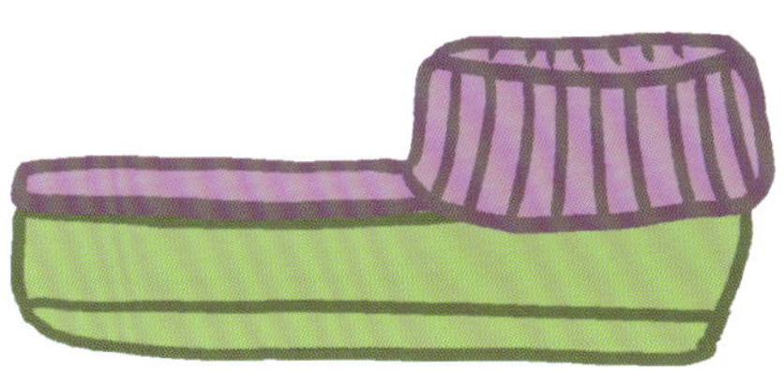

4. Then work your ribbing and you have a completed slipper!

project 12

KENNEDY

Amigurumi Pincushion

project 12:
AMIGURUMI PINCUSHION

Amigurumi is a word of Japanese origin used to describe any number of small, three-dimensional, crocheted stuffed objects, often creatures or toys. It is a hugely popular style of crochet, and you may very well want to make these for yourself or be asked to make them for others. To get you started, we've designed this adorable pincushion, which will familiarize you with some of the common techniques used in amigurumi, including making 3-D shapes, stuffing objects, and sewing 3-D shapes together.

note: If working with such a small hook and thinner yarn daunts you, you can also make this with thicker yarn and a larger hook to make a pillow. Just check the recommended hook sizes on your yarn's label and try using the smallest size recommended. Your fabric should be very dense so as not to let your stuffing out. If your fabric is not dense enough, keep trying with a smaller hook size until it feels right.

top tip!

When sewing the pieces of your flower together after they are all crocheted, you might want to use locking stitch markers or safety pins to secure each petal to the center of your flower to keep it in place while you sew. Only secure one petal at a time, so you have as much space as possible for sewing. Evenly spacing the petals might feel a little tricky, but determining how much space each petal takes up and affixing them to the center will keep you on the right path.

notes on construction:

This pincushion is made by working each three-dimensional part of the flower separately and then sewing them together. First, the center is made by working a tube in the round. Each petal is made from three pieces that are sewn together. All pieces are then filled with toy stuffing and sewn together.

techniques you need to know:

- Single crochet (see page 15)
- Double crochet (see page 46)
- Half double crochet (see page 61)
- Treble crochet (see page 100)
- Magic ring (see page 64)
- Slip stitch seam (see page 23)

techniques introduced:

- Sewing 3-D shapes together (see pages 174–175)

pattern 12

KENNEDY
Amigurumi Pincushion

One size: 12.5 cm/5" diameter x 4 cm/1½" depth

Yarn: Scheepjes Catona (fingering/4-ply weight; 100% mercerized cotton; 125 m/137 yds per 50-g/1.75-oz ball)

Shades:

Yarn A: Saffron (249); 1 ball

Yarn B: Apricot (524); 1 ball

Yarn C: Old Rose (408); 1 ball

OR approx:

Yarn A: 10 m/11 yds of fingering/4-ply weight yarn

Yarn B: 16 m/18 yds of fingering/4-ply weight yarn

Yarn C: 16 m/18 yds of fingering/4-ply weight yarn

Gauge: 25 sts & 25 rows = 10 cm/4" in single crochet using 2.5 mm hook

Hook: US C-2/2.75 mm

Always use a hook size that will result in the correct gauge.

Notions: Locking stitch marker, tapestry needle, toy stuffing

PATTERN

FLOWER CENTER

Using Yarn A, make magic ring. You will now begin working a spiral in the round.

Round 1 (RS): 6sc into magic ring, pull tail firmly to close ring, PM in st to indicate beginning of round. *6 sts*

Continue moving marker to new first st on each round.

Round 2 (inc): 2sc in each sc to end. *12 sts*

Round 3 (inc): [1sc in next sc, 2sc in next sc] to end. *18 sts*

Round 4: 1sc in each sc to end.

Rep Round 4 until piece measures approx 3 cm/1¼" from the last increase round.

Round 5: [1sc in next sc, sc2tog] to end. *12 sts*

Fill shape with toy stuffing.

Round 6: [Sc2tog] to end. *6 sts*

Cut yarn, leaving a long tail. Thread yarn onto tapestry needle and sew opening closed by working into the remaining stitches and pulling tightly to close. Insert the threaded needle into the shape and draw through to the opposite side to hide the tail, cutting away any excess length.

FLOWER PETALS
(make 3 each in Yarns B and C)

top/bottom of petal
(make 2 for each flower petal)

Make magic ring.

Row 1: 3sc into magic ring, pull tail firmly to close ring, turn. *3 sts*

Row 2: Ch1 (counts as first sc throughout), [1sc in next sc] twice, turn.

Row 3: Ch1, 1sc in same sc, 1sc in next sc, 2sc in next sc, turn. *5 sts*

Row 4: Ch1, 1sc in each sc to end, turn.

Row 5: Ch1, 1sc in same sc, 1sc in each sc to last st, 2sc in last sc, turn. *7 sts*

Row 6: Ch1, 1sc in each sc to end, turn.

Rows 7–9: Rep Row 6 a further 3 times.

Row 10: Ch1, 1hdc in next sc, 1dc in next sc, 1tr in next sc, 1dc in next sc, 1hdc in next sc, 1sc in last sc.

Cut yarn and fasten off.

sides of petal (make 1 for each flower petal):

Ch9.

Row 1: 1sc in 2nd ch from hook (missed 1-ch does not count as st), 1sc in each ch to end, turn. *8 sts*

Row 2: Ch1 (counts as first sc), 1sc in each sc to end, turn.

Repeat Row 2 a further 26 times.

Fasten off.

FINISHING

petal assembly

note: Right and wrong sides are not crucial here as the fabric is reversible. See also Assembling Flower Petals, page 174.

Using the slip stitch crochet method, seam together one long edge of the Sides of Petal piece to the Top of Petal, starting at the tip of the Top of Petal and working the strip all the way around the edge until it reaches the tip once again.

Repeat using the other long edge of the Sides of Petal piece and the Bottom of Petal. You will now have an unstuffed, three-dimensional petal. Leave the opening of the short edges of the Sides of Petal strip unseamed.

Repeat to create the five remaining petals.

flower assembly

note: See also Sewing on Petals, page 175.

Once the center of the flower and all petals are completed, turn each petal inside out so the seams are hidden inside the petals. Tuck any remaining yarn ends inside as well. Stuff each petal generously with toy stuffing. Using a tapestry needle, sew the open edges of each petal to the center of the flower, ensuring the petals are equally spaced. The petals will be snug, and sewing will require a bit more effort as each petal is added and there is less space. Insert any remaining yarn ends into the pincushion and trim as needed.

a. Diameter: 12.5 cm/5"
b. Height: 4 cm/1½"

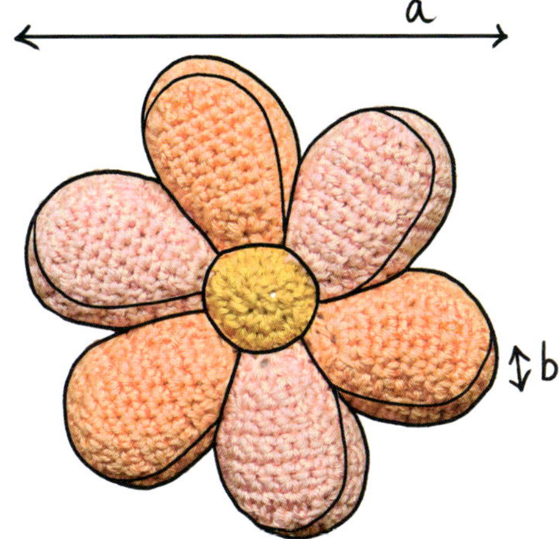

using stitch markers in the round

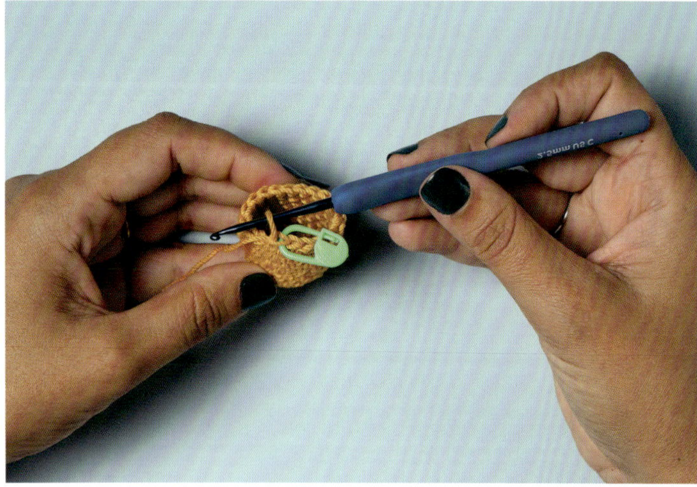

Using a stitch marker for marking the beginning of a round is both easy and essential. Without a stitch marker, it is extremely difficult to locate the first and last stitches of your rounds. Simply place a marker in the first stitch of your round when you first join it to work in the round. Work around each stitch as directed until you arrive back at the marker. Remove the marker to work into the first stitch for your next round and place it on the new first stitch as soon as it is worked.

working rounds with stuffing inserted

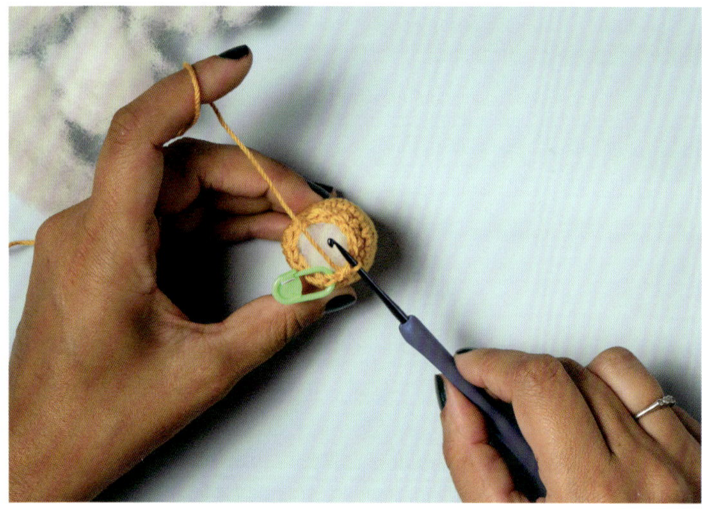

When making stuffed objects, you will often make a part of that object to the point where you add stuffing and then continue making the remainder of the object until it is closed up. To do this, simply continue working into your stitches as normal, tucking in the stuffing where necessary as you go.

sewing openings closed

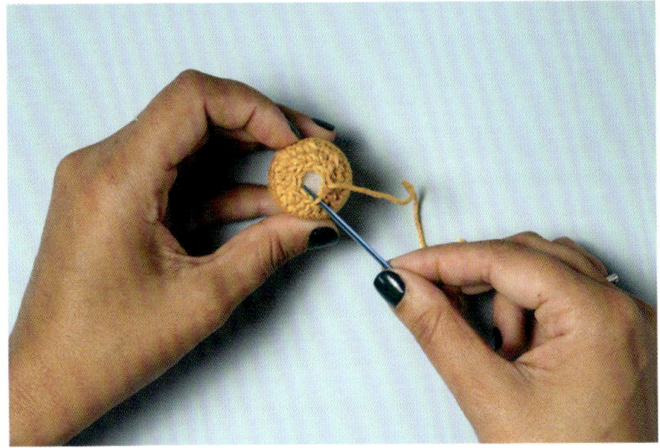

1. Once the crocheting for a piece is complete, fasten off your yarn in the usual way, leaving an extra-long tail. Thread the tail onto a tapestry needle, and then insert the needle into the uppermost strand of the stitch closest to the tail.

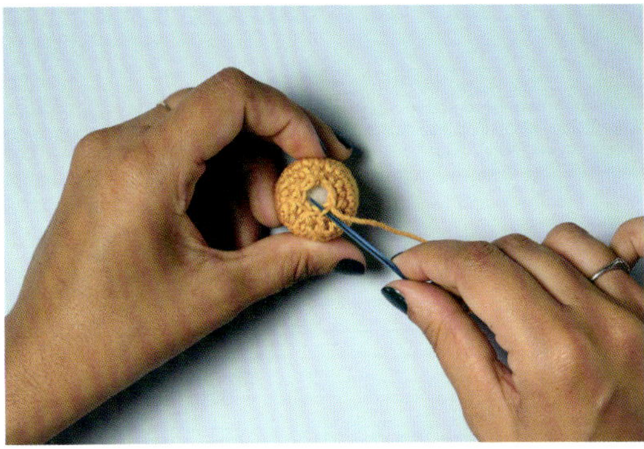

2. Draw the yarn through and insert the needle into the next stitch the same way. Continue to sew through the uppermost strand of each stitch around the opening.

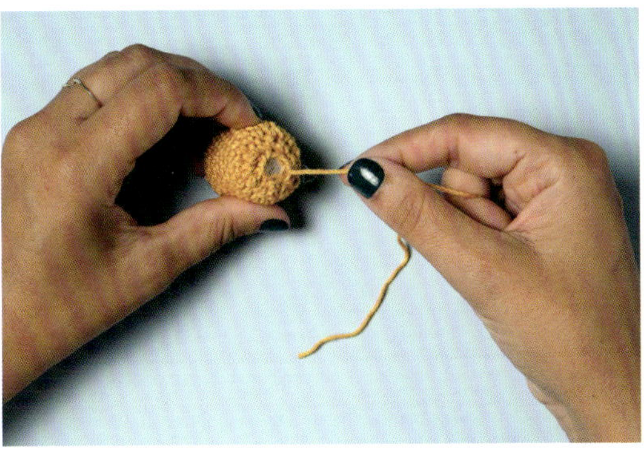

3. Pull the strand tightly to draw the opening closed.

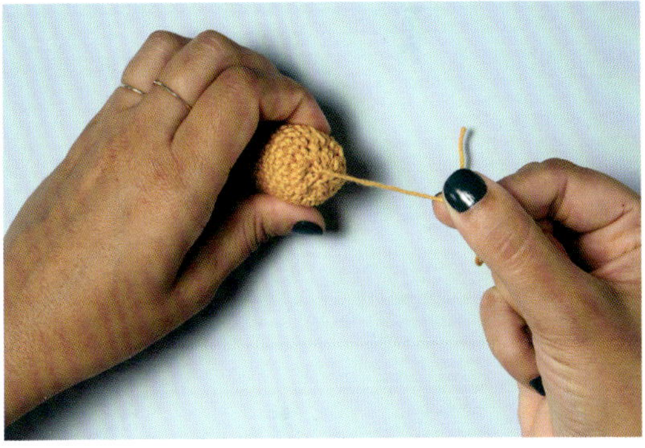

4. Pull until it is completely closed.

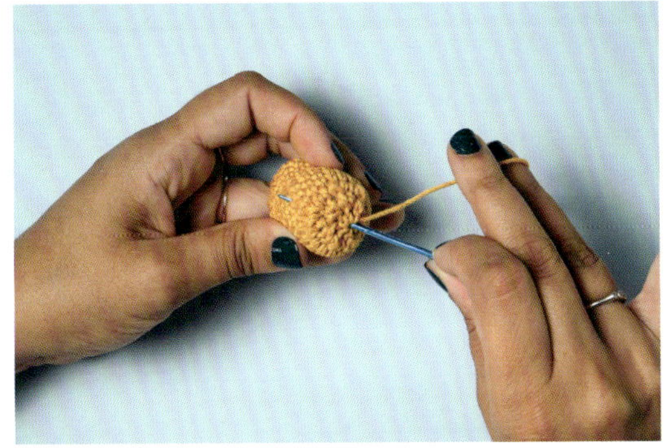

5. With the tail threaded onto the needle, insert the needle into the middle of the opening and push through until it comes out of the side of the piece.

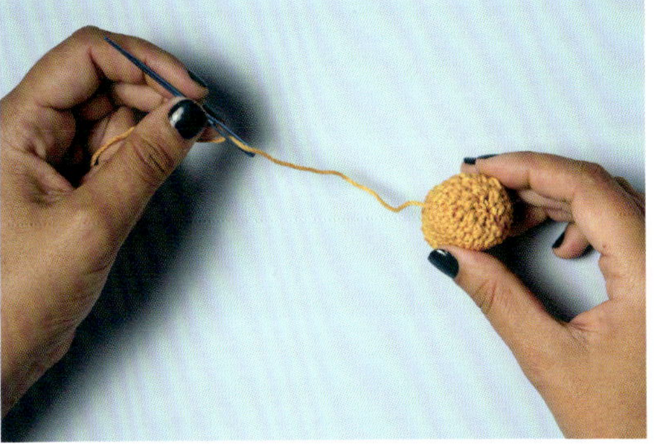

6. Draw the tail completely though the stuffed object. Snip any excess quite close, and then squeeze the stuffed object to allow the tail to be drawn inside.

assembling flower petals

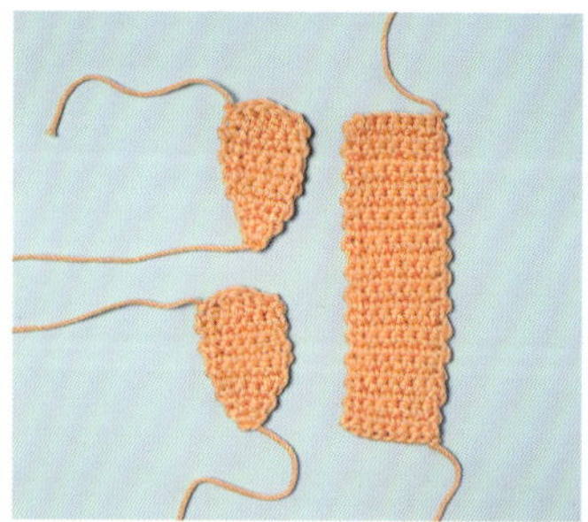

1. When assembling each three-dimensional flower petal, you will have three pieces: a Top of Petal and a Bottom of Petal (which are identical) and a Side of Petal piece.

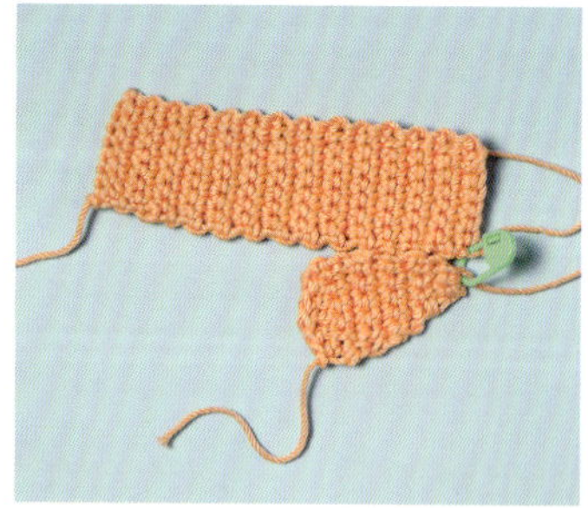

2. To assemble, first you will seam the Top of Petal to one long edge of the Side of Petal. You may want to use locking stitch markers to keep the pieces aligned.

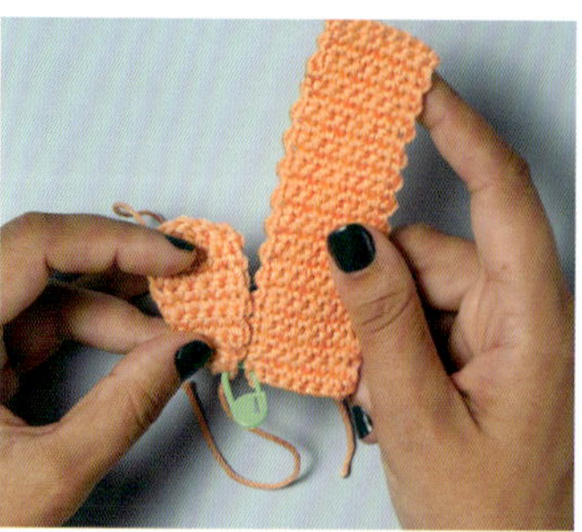

3. The Side of Petal piece is going to be seamed all the way around the Top of Petal piece.

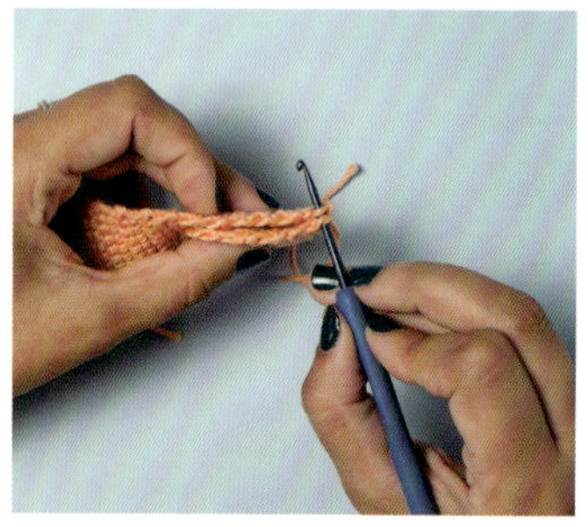

4. With the two pieces sandwiched together, insert your hook into the edge of both layers.

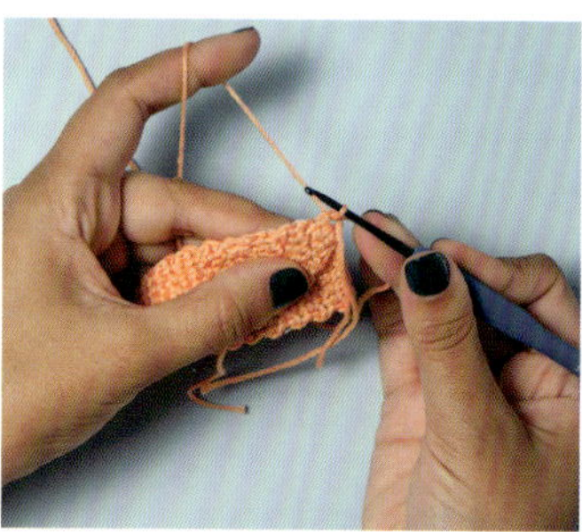

5. Draw up a loop through both layers.

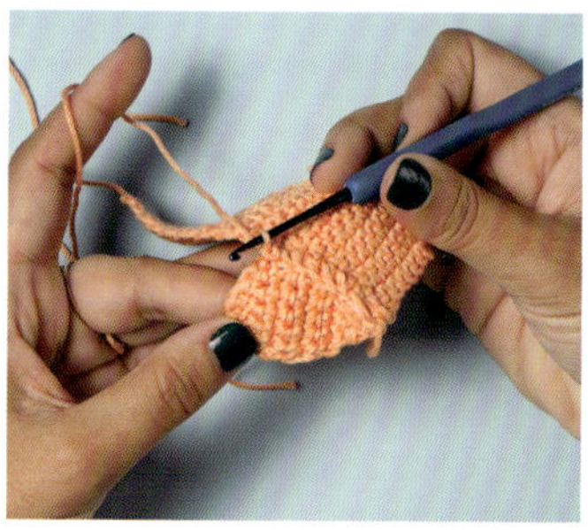

6. Work a slip stitch seam (see page 23) along one side of the Top of Petal.

7. Continue to work the slip stitch seam all the way around the Top of Petal piece, ensuring the Side of Petal strip is evenly distributed around the Top of Petal. You may have to readjust, but the process will become more straightforward with each petal you make. Cut yarn and fasten off.

8. This photo shows the Side of Petal completely attached to the Top of Petal. Repeat the process on the other side using the Bottom of Petal piece. Turn the petal inside out so the seam and any yarn tails are hidden. Stuff the petal with toy stuffing, but do not seam the remaining opening closed.

sewing on petals

1. Once all six petals are made, use a tapestry needle to sew the open edges of each petal to the Flower Center. Arrange the petals so that they are equally spaced. You can attach the petals with locking stitch markers or safety pins while you sew them on, if desired.

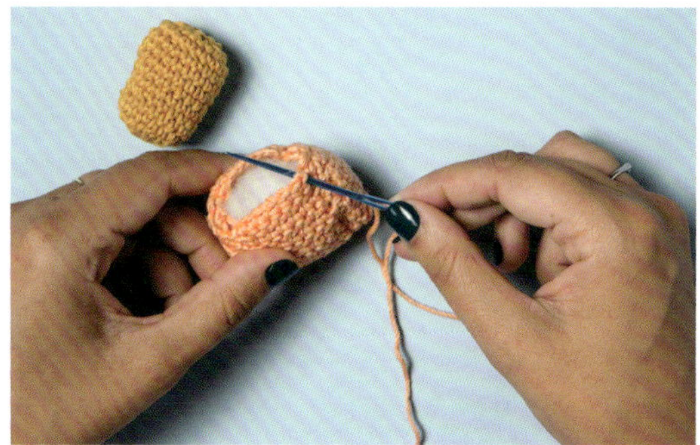

2. Using a tapestry needle threaded with a 25 cm/10" length of yarn matching the petal, insert the needle into the open edge of the petal.

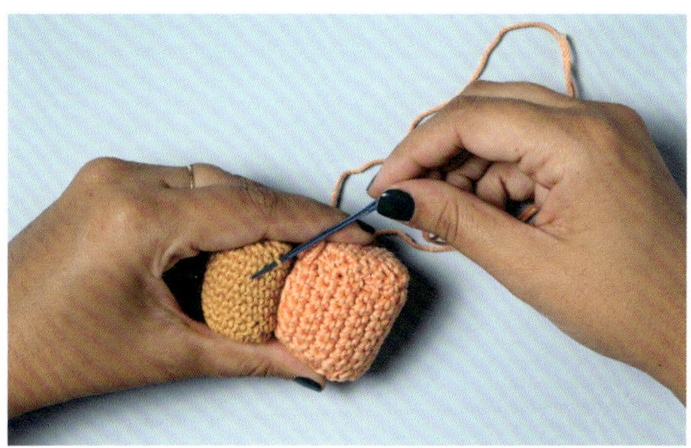

3. Then insert the needle into the Flower Center at the place where you want it to attach.

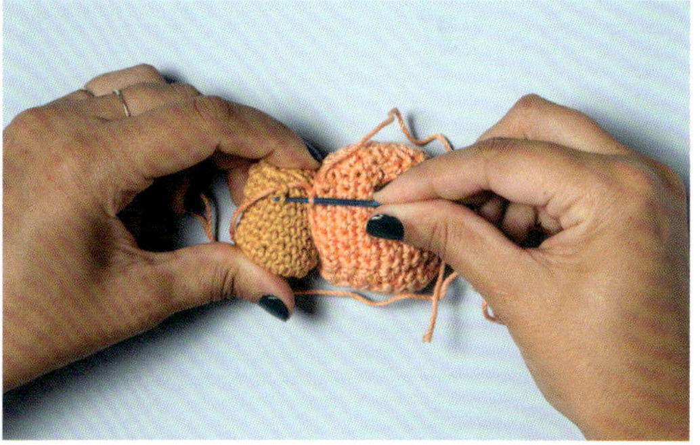

4. Continue in this way all the way down one side of the petal opening.

5. Your petal should already feel quite securely sewn to the Flower Center on one side.

6. Continue sewing the petal to the Flower Center all the way around the petal opening. The petal is now firmly attached. Draw the remaining yarn tail through to the inside of the object and cut any excess. Repeat for the five remaining petals.

PART 3

COMMON MISTAKES & CARING FOR YOUR MAKES

We can pretty much guarantee that in every project you make, you'll mess up. Even when you've been crocheting for months or years. We certainly still find we've made mistakes when we crochet, just as every other crocheter out there does. So, what do we do?

If you're already a knitter, you might be used to picking up "dropped" stitches that have unraveled. Great news! You can't really drop crochet stitches, because they are pretty much all secure except for the live stitch on your hook. On the flip side, in crochet, if you realize you've made an error a few rows back, it's likely that the only way to fix it is to undo your stitches back to that point. To undo your stitches, all you have to do is remove your hook from the live stitch and pull the yarn until all the stitches are unraveled up to and including the error. You can then place the current live stitch on your hook and begin to work again from the point before your mistake.

To avert the tedium of ripping out your hard-earned stitches, you'll want to take these preventative measures to avoid common mistakes.

COMMON MISTAKES

inserting your hook incorrectly

Meghan distinctly remembers making her first project and going only under one loop of her stitches instead of two. Unless specified to create a certain feature or look, you should always insert your hook under both strands of the V that appears at the top of the row of stitches you are working into. (This does not apply to when you work into a chain.)

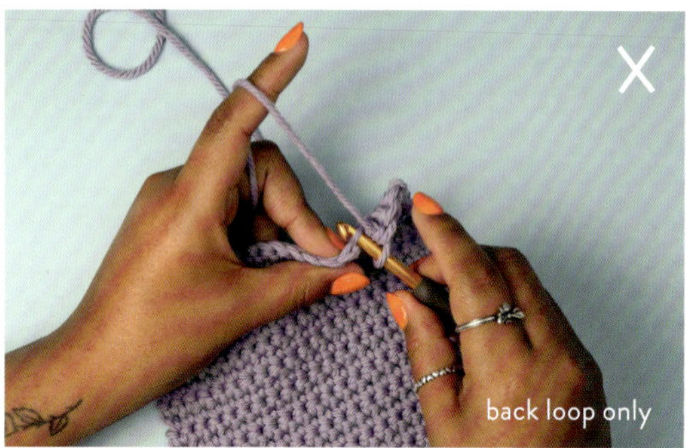

back loop only

front loop only

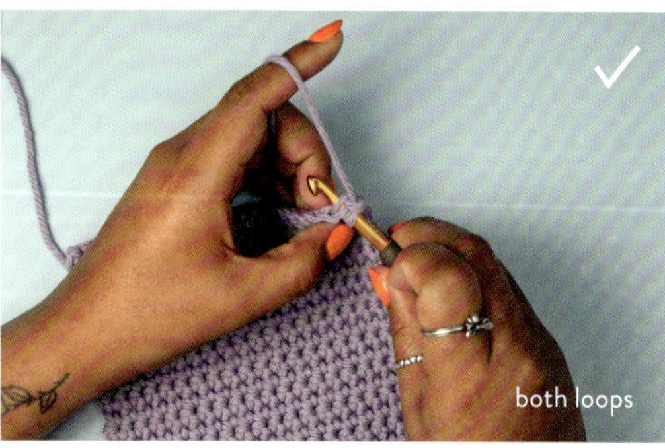

both loops

Working into the back loop only (BLO) or front loop only (FLO) are legitimate techniques. But be aware that unless specifically called for, you should be working into both loops of a stitch.

working too many stitches into a row

Crochet stitches can be hard to count sometimes, especially at the beginning and end of a row, where turning chain stitches may be confusing. To ensure you know exactly where your row begins and ends, consider placing a removable stitch marker on the stitch immediately once you've completed it. In other words, work the first stitch and insert a marker into it right away so that when you return to it at the end of the next row, you can identify it immediately.

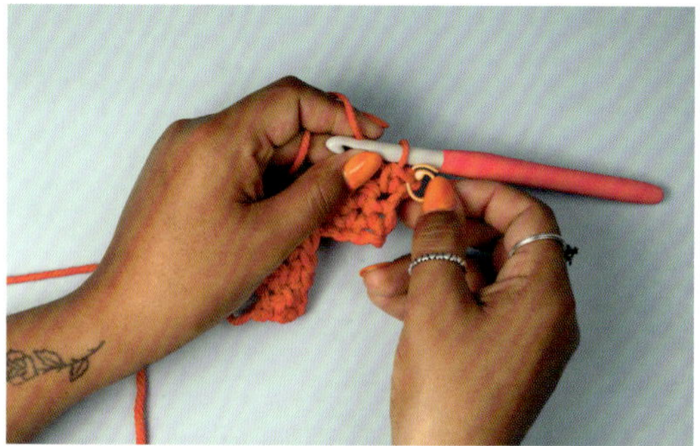

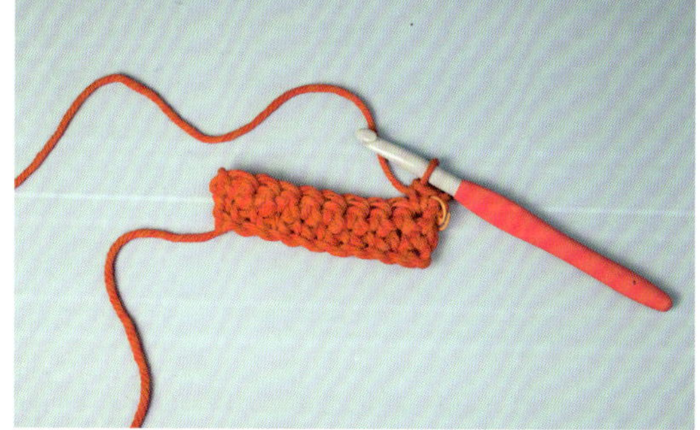

turning chain cheat sheet

One common reason that a piece of fabric mysteriously grows is because a crocheter accidentally works into the first stitch in a row. This stitch is usually skipped when the turning chain is counted as a stitch, so if you work into it, you'll end up creating an additional stitch in that row. This technique can be used for purposeful increases (see page 90), but you only want to do it if you mean to.

Here's a handy-dandy cheat sheet to remind you which stitch to work into after your turning chain for the four stitches we cover in this book: single crochet, half double crochet, double crochet, and treble crochet. The arrows show which stitch you work into after working your turning chain—remember that for single crochet your turning chain doesn't count as a stitch, whereas for the other stitches it does!

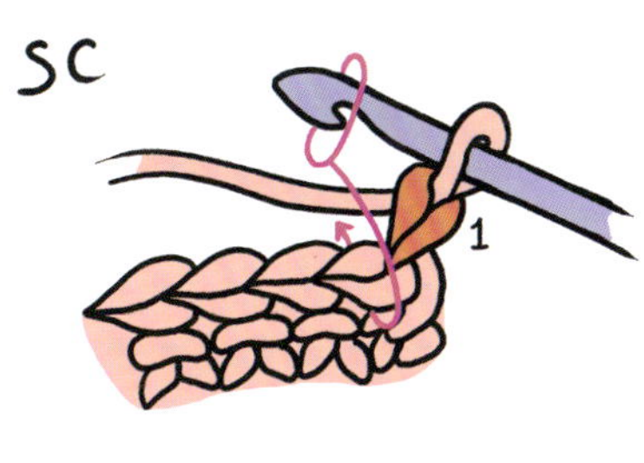

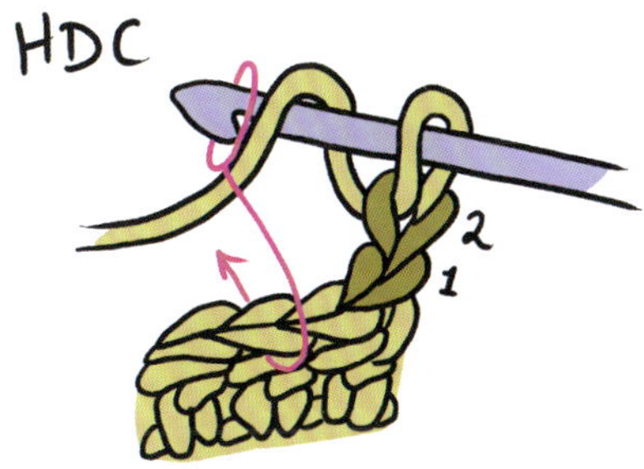

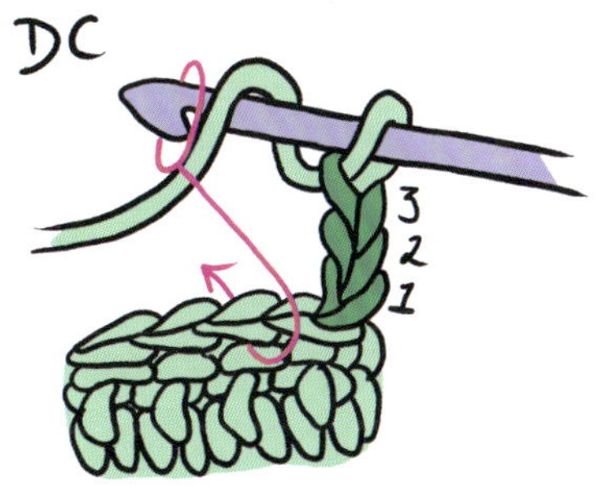

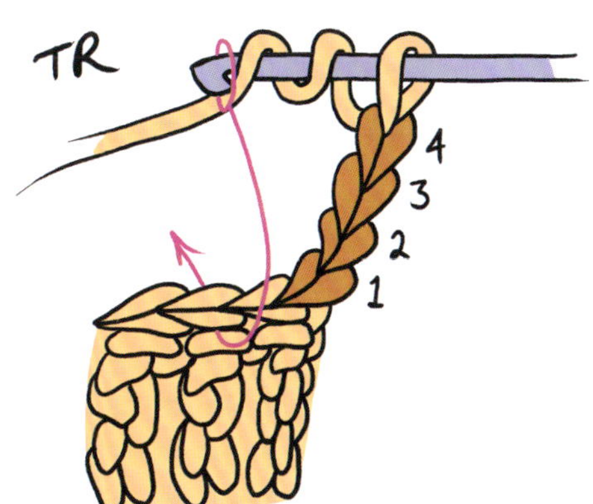

CARING FOR YOUR MAKES

Once you've completed a project, you get to wear it! And then wash it, store it, and give it some general maintenance and TLC. Here are a few of our tips for keeping your crochet shipshape for years to come.

washing

Some crochet pieces, like a cowl or mittens, may rarely need washing. But even for these creations, there's always the chance of a spilled cup of hot chocolate, or a bus driving through a dirty puddle at just the wrong moment. For hand-crocheted items, washing is essentially the same process as blocking (described in Part 1 on page 30). Even when yarn is marketed as being "superwash," meaning it is machine washable, we are fans of hand-washing. Many washing machines have knitwear cycles, but we've seen far too many heartbreaking accidents to recommend relying on this. Warm water, strong detergents, and the normal friction of the washing machine can easily shrink—or worse, felt—your item. We can't bear to think of you losing your beautiful project that took so many hours to make, so why chance it? The exception to this would be projects in cotton or linen, which can often benefit from a machine wash and dry, which can both soften up and tighten stitches that have become stretched out from wear.

To recap, washing or blocking your crocheted items involves giving them a lukewarm, sudsy bath using a no-rinse wool wash, gently squeezing out the water, and laying the piece flat to dry, pinning if necessary to get it to the specified measurements. Most yarn shops sell a no-rinse wool wash. If you can't get to a shop or find there are too many choices, then gentle Eucalan is a great brand to start with.

storing

Larger crocheted items are best kept folded in a drawer. Much as we'd love to see a beautiful lineup of sweaters in our wardrobes, hangers are really not their friends. Hangers will put an unnecessary strain on the shoulders of garments and cause the weight of the yarn to stretch the entire piece.

Many crocheters are waging a constant battle with moths. If you live in a region rife with moths, consider using a wool wash with lavender, or investing in sachets meant to deter moths. Moths especially love wooly garments that the wearer has sweat into; all the more reason to keep your pieces nice and wash them now and again. If you have a very serious moth problem, you may want to store your crochet pieces (and even your yarn) in airtight plastic bags or containers. You can amuse yourself by organizing them by color or thickness of yarn—or is it just us that finds this fun?

de-pilling

Over time, you may notice little bobbly pills appearing on your crochet items, especially in places where there is extra friction, like on the underside of sleeves, where your arms rub against your body. The softer your yarn is, the more likely pills will happen. Don't stress though: Your sweater isn't ruined, it just needs some love. There are a number of handy tools you can use to remove the pills. Battery-operated pill shavers are great, as are tools like the Gleener that are marketed specifically to crafters. In a pinch, a razor will do the trick; just be careful.

PART 4

WHERE TO NEXT?

Whether you've completed a few or all of the projects in this book or are just using it as a reference, we hope we've given you a good foundation and introduction to the amazing world of crochet. As you continue on your crochet journey, every project you make is going to build on and reinforce your knowledge and confidence. We're so excited for you to grow and savor every stitch and hope that it gives you as much joy as it gives us.

You'll soon find (if you haven't already) that there is a HUGE world of crochet content on social media. The crochet community spans everything from amigurumi aficionados to large-scale artists to slow-fashion devotees. We hope you find your people, enjoy being inspired, and feel like you can call yourself a Crocheter with a capital C.

onward

We're going to go ahead and assume you want to keep crocheting and trying new projects and patterns. So how do you decide what to make next? There will be things you want to make, and things you feel ready to make. Try to find a marriage of the two.

The website ravelry.com is an almost infinite directory of both crochet and knitting patterns and allows them to be searched by a huge number of attributes, including difficulty, yarn type, availability (downloadable or in print), neckline style, fit, and so on. You can also see projects other people of all shapes and sizes have made from a pattern. If that feels overwhelming, try following a crochet influencer whose style you like to see what they are making and wait to find out what inspires you.

If you're feeling ambitious and want to try intricate crochet lace for your next project, we're here for it. And if you want to keep making new versions of projects you've already made from this book, we're here for that too. Crochet is not a race, but if it were, slow and steady would certainly win.

Whatever you decide to do next, the main thing we hope for you is that you enjoy it. Revel in every stitch, let the soft fibers of the yarn soothe you, and wear and use the things you've made with pride. After all, your warm, lively, human hands did something no machine has ever done—crochet. You're a wonder!

ABBREVIATIONS

Please note that this book uses US crochet terminology. For more information, see page 21.

beg	Beginning
BLO	Back loop only
ch	Chain
dc	Double crochet
dec	Decrease
FLO	Front loop only
foll	Follow(s)/Following
hdc	Half double crochet
inc	Increase
MC	Main color
patt	Pattern (i.e., work in pattern)
PM	Place marker
prev	Previous
rem	Remain(s)/Remaining
rep	Repeat
RS	Right side of fabric
sc	Single crochet
sk	Skip
sl st	Slip stitch
sp	Space
st(s)	Stitch(es)
tog	Together
tr	Treble crochet
WS	Wrong side of fabric
yo	Yarn over hook

HANDY CONVERSIONS

yarn

Here are some frequently used names for yarn weights and their overseas equivalents.

US	UK
Lace Weight	Lace Weight
Fingering/Sock	4-Ply
Sport	Between a Heavy 4-Ply and Light DK
DK (Double Knit)/ Light Worsted	DK (Double Knit)
Worsted	Aran
Bulky	Chunky
Super Bulky	Super Chunky

CROCHET LINGO

Phrases and abbreviations you can start using online and IRL like a pro.

CAL
Crochet-Along. When a group of crocheters make the same project or similar projects at the same time and share progress with one another. Often hosted at local yarn shops or on social media platforms.

Errata
We all make mistakes! Errata are published corrections to the instructions in a crochet pattern. Usually, a pattern designer or publisher will have a page on their website that lists updates or corrections. It's always worth checking before you start working on a pattern to see if there are any errata—hopefully there aren't, but if there are, checking will save you a lot of time in the long run.

FO
Finished Object. This refers to a finished crochet project.

Frog
To frog is to unravel part or all of a project. It got this name because undoing your work is also called "ripping out," and "rip it" sounds like *ribbit* (the noise that frogs make).

LYS
Local Yarn Shop/Store

Startitis
Beginning several projects in quick succession but not making progress on them before starting the next.

Stash
Yarn awaiting a future project.

UFO
Unfinished Object (see FO at left).

WIP
Work in Progress.

Yarn Barf
A clump of yarn that comes out of a new ball of yarn when you pull from the center of the ball.

Yarn Chicken
When you are coming to the end of a project and running out of yarn, you are playing yarn chicken. Will the crocheter win or will the yarn run out?

YARN SUPPORT

Here's a comprehensive list of yarns we used in this book and where to find them. If you're not able to use the yarns suggested, have a look at our substitution guide (see following section) for help choosing an alternative.

De Rerum Natura
Cyrano
dererumnatura.fr

Hobbii
Pom Pom x Hobbii Garland and Rainbow 8/6
hobbii.com

Kelbourne Woolens
Mojave and Germantown Bulky
kelbournewoolens.com

Kremke Soul Wool
The Merry Merino 70 GOTS
soul-wool.com

Manos del Uruguay
Cardo and Ideal
manos.uy/yarns

Purl Soho
Cotton Chirp and Plein Air
purlsoho.com

Ritual Dyes
Undine DK
ritualdyes.com

Rosa Pomar
Cobertor
retrosaria.rosapomar.com

Scheepjes
Catona
scheepjes.com

SUBSTITUTING YARNS

There are many reasons to try a different yarn than the one called for in the pattern: geography, color, and fiber are all good reasons to deviate from what's prescribed. Cotton is very traditional for many crocheted items, but you certainly aren't limited to using only cotton, and crochet can be beautiful in many different fibers. Here's our handy guide to changing things up.

1. Use the meter per gram rule, also known as the yards per ounce rule. Have a look at your pattern and see how many meters there are in the ball. As an example, there might be 80 meters/87½ yards per 50-gram/1.75-ounce ball. When choosing a substitute, go for a yarn that has a very similar number of meters per gram, or yards per ounce, as the case may be.

2. Think about usage. It's unlikely that you'll want cotton mittens, because cotton will stretch and won't keep you very warm. So, think about where and how your crocheted item will be used. If you're making a sweater for your friend in Norway, it's a good idea to use warm wool. If you're making a cardigan for your cousin who lives in Florida, consider a cotton blend.

3. Give thought to drape and weight. The easiest thing to do when substituting yarns is to stick to the same fiber content as the original. You'll find fiber content information on the yarn label. Wool usually has springy properties, whereas an alpaca and silk blend will usually be drapey and can stretch with wear. This can be beautiful when the pattern is designed to accommodate drape. But if you swap wool for alpaca in a pattern that doesn't accommodate it, you might find yourself with a cardigan much longer than you intended it to be after a few wears. Eventually you will become more familiar with how different fibers behave, but if you want to play it safe for now, go with the recommended fiber to avoid unpleasant surprises.

ACKNOWLEDGMENTS

The making of *Crochet How* has been a wild ride, and we couldn't have done it without the help and support of many, many people! First, we would like to thank our editor, Shawna Mullen, who believed in us enough to ask us to write this book and has been patient and supportive throughout the process. The whole Abrams team have been wonderful, all adding their expertise to the book, for which we are very grateful. We are especially thankful to Jenice Kim for her beautiful layout design.

Kennedy Berry was a font of knowledge and insight, and took the beautiful tutorial photos you'll find throughout with Gavriella Treminio as the hook-holding hands! Salsabil Morrison as always saw our vision and turned it into reality, bringing her own eye and flair to the modeled photos in this book. Sara Farrag-Kramer and Yly Tolentino wore and carried the crochet pieces with pizazz. Ashley Kay Searles was a wiz with hair and makeup, and Helgate Pottery allowed us to use their space before it was kitted out as a ceramics studio. Atwin and Beyond Nine let us borrow the gorgeous clothes styled with the crochet pieces, and Daisy Elsom and Zahra Zubaidah were essential in making the shoot run smoothly.

Edie Eckman did an incredible job of finessing the patterns and making sure our tutorials and text were as clear as possible. Jemima Bicknell and Laura Chau worked hard to turn draft patterns into something that made good sense!

We'd like to thank two members of our Pom Pom family, Amy Collins and Sophie Heathscott, who read early drafts and offered their invaluable feedback and unwavering support. Sophie also made many of the samples you see in this book.

Thanks too to Meghan's local yarn shop, Knit ATX, for their cheerleading and for loaning us the swift and winder used in the winding tutorial. Meghan would like to thank her family for putting up with long hours and yarn in every corner of the house, along with a special mention for Jane, her grandmother's neighbor and incredible lace-maker, who taught her (a hopeless left-hander!) to crochet among the palm trees and lizards in Goa, India.

Lydia would like to thank her mum, Sarah, for stepping in to provide (a lot of!) last-minute childcare in the run up to the photoshoot and for always being supportive of Pom Pom, and Dan, parent and partner extraordinaire. Thanks to Lydia's dad, Jeremy, for his enthusiasm for creative projects, and to Diana for childcare and encouragement. Lydia would also like to thank Arman, who lent his Huion pad to speed up the process of creating the illustrations; the whole Elio studio gang for morale-boosting; and Amy Allcroft, who helped with weaving in ends at the last minute.

Lastly, thanks to Juju Vail, who has always been our craft mentor, for her sage advice, sample making, weaving in ends, and extra help at the shoot.

And of course, a huge thank-you to you for buying this book! We hope that crochet brings as much joy and color into your life as it has to ours.

INDEX

Page references in *italics* refer to illustrations or images.

Editor: Shawna Mullen
Designer: Jenice Kim
Managing Editor: Marie Oishi
Production Manager: Sarah Masterson Hally
Tech Editor: Edie Eckman

Library of Congress Control Number: 2025937178

ISBN: 978-1-4197-8002-8
eISBN: 978-8-88707-580-8

Text copyright © 2025 Meghan Fernandes and Lydia Gluck
Illustrations copyright © 2025 Lydia Gluck
Tutorial photographs copyright © Kennedy Berry
All other photographs copyright © Salsabil Morrison

Cover © 2025 Abrams

Published in 2025 by Abrams, an imprint of ABRAMS. All rights reserved. No portion of this book may be reproduced, stored in a retrieval system, or transmitted in any form or by any means, mechanical, electronic, photocopying, recording, or otherwise, without written permission from the publisher.

Printed and bound in China
10 9 8 7 6 5 4 3 2 1

Abrams books are available at special discounts when purchased in quantity for premiums and promotions as well as fundraising or educational use. Special editions can also be created to specification. For details, contact specialsales@abramsbooks.com or the address below.

Abrams® is a registered trademark of Harry N. Abrams, Inc.

ABRAMS is represented in the UK and Europe by Abrams & Chronicle Books, 1 West Smithfield, London EC1A 9JU and Média-Participations, 57 rue Gaston Tessier, 75166 Paris, France.
abramsandchronicle.co.uk and
media-participations.com
info@abramsandchronicle.co.uk

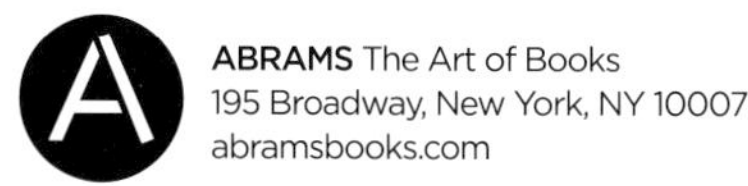